SATISFACTION
THE STORY OF
Mick Jagger

PROTEUS BOOKS is an imprint of
The Proteus Publishing Group

United States
PROTEUS PUBLISHING COMPANY, INC.
9 West 57th Street, Suite 4503,
New York, NY 10019

distributed by:
CHERRY LANE BOOKS COMPANY, INC.
PO Box No. 430,
Port Chester, NY 10573

United Kingdom
PROTEUS BOOKS LIMITED
Bremar House, Sale Place,
London W2 1PT

ISBN 0 86276 135 2 (paperback)
ISBN 0 86276 136 0 (hardback)

First published in U.S. 1984
First published in U.K. 1984

Photocredits:
Ace Photo Agency, Alpha Press Agency, Cyrus Andrews,
Aquarius Literary Agency, Rob Burt Collection, Ian Dickson,
Keystone/CLI, Bob Leafe, Barry Plummer, David Redfern,
Photography, Rex Features, Mick Rock, Pennie Smith,
Frank Spooner Pictures, Star File, Syndication International.

Editor: Kay Rowley
Designed by: Jill Mumford
Typeset by: SX Composing Ltd., Rayleigh, Essex
Printed in Great Britain
by Blantyre Printing & Binding Co., Glasgow

SATISFACTION
THE STORY OF
MICK JAGGER
BY JOHN ALDRIDGE

PROTEUS BOOKS
London/New York

Allow me to introduce myself

The Rolling Stones have drawn their strength from the personality, the quick wit and the nous of Mick Jagger, and the musical dexterity of Keith Richard. That is an over-simplification, but it nevertheless conveys the correct impression.

Certainly, had the group contained other members demanding to be equally as influential as those two then it would have splintered long ago. But it was always moulded by the special chemistry between Jagger and Richard. On the whole, the others were content with their supporting roles.

Richard, of course, has had his periods of incapacitation. Jagger has always been solidly in charge, and certainly all the administrative and managerial duties concerning the group have devolved upon him. But more than that, he has kept the group together by force of personality, and has ensured that it retained its position of pre-eminence in the entertainment world. That is his achievement.

Being a Rolling Stone has been Mick Jagger's entire adult life – after all, his membership of the group actually preceded the completion of the formal education studies. Thus, to tell his story is to tell the story of The Rolling Stones. It is impossible to conceive of either without the other.

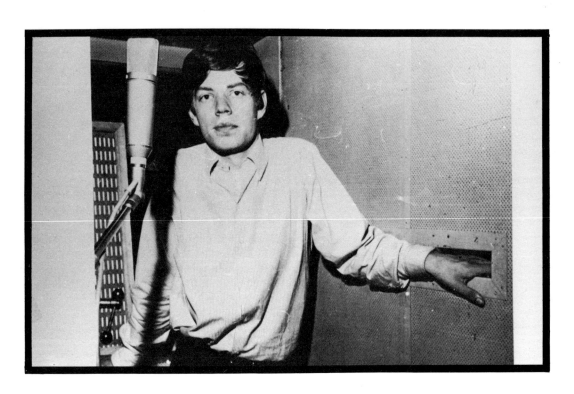

Jagger in a recording studio, 1963.

"I did not have," Mick Jagger once admitted, "a raving adolescence". Indeed not. He was born in Dartford, Kent, on July 26, 1943 into a moderately well-off family. It was not a prosperous upbringing, but neither – once his father Basil ('Joe') Jagger had landed a job as physical education instructor at Dartford Grammar School – was it a difficult one.

The family then moved to the village of Wilmington, into a white stucco house with apple trees in the garden, where Mick and his younger brother Chris used to romp together. On the whole, then, a relatively comfortable beginning in life, in a part of the South-East hinterland of London which was itself traditionally immune from the winds of social and economic ill-fortune that periodically ripped through Northern regions.

Mick's school career was not a chequered one – not, at least, in any sense that an aspiring rock 'n' roll star would have considered meaningful. He was essentially dutiful, his natural adolescent rebelliousness tempered by a sense of scholastic discipline. Like most children with parents within the education system, he applied himself to his studies, diligently doing his homework. However, his father's professional concerns notwithstanding, Jagger was not inclined to take sport seriously. He did have a naturally athletic physique, and this was one area in which he was considered unambitious.

But while he had no appetite for sport, he was soon showing an interest in music – listening to Radio Luxembourg (at that time the solitary source for UK teenagers of popular music in the evenings) and playing, as was the fashion of the day, in sundry impromptu skiffle groups.

Such concerns, however, were not allowed to disrupt his studies and, having flirted with the idea of becoming a journalist, Jagger went on to study politics and economics at the London School of Economics, one of the UK's most prestigious educational establishments outside of Oxford and Cambridge. He began what was supposed to have been a three-year course there in October 1961, with the view that he should eventually take up accountancy. It might well be pointed out that he ended up a long way from that allotted profession; equally, it is also worth pointing out that ever since he has handled all financial affairs with the shrewdness of a first-class accountant.

Most commentators agree on the first incident in the chapter of desultory events that led to the formation of The Rolling Stones: the chance meeting, on a suburban train somewhere between Dartford and London Bridge, of Jagger and Keith Richard. They had known each other some ten years earlier when both were pupils at Wentworth Primary School, but had lost touch when Richard's family moved to a new housing estate across town.

It was the summer of 1961. Jagger was clutching a number of imported R&B albums, and Richard was carrying his trusty guitar: it was quickly apparent that they shared musical interests – in particular, both were fervent disciples of Chuck Berry. Subsequent conversation revealed that they also had a friend in common – Dick Taylor, who had been at Dartford Grammar School with Mick, and was by then at Sidcup Art College with Keith.

By that time Jagger and Taylor were playing their own R&B in a casual ensemble called Little Boy Blue and the Blue Boys. Richard was a natural and an immediate recruit. This marked the beginning of an association that has been flourishing ever since. Jagger and Richard immediately struck up a firm friendship. An instinctive creative rapport was soon to follow.

Richard was different to the other Stones. He did not distinguish himself academically, and neither was he ever interested in full-time employment. The steps the other four took towards a career in music were usually calculated ones; Richard was the one who, having made an emotional commitment to music, burned his bridges behind him.

He attended Dartford Technical School, an essentially shy boy who, towards the end of his school days, adopted the teddy-boy fashions and anti-authoritarian attitudes that first surfaced in the late fifties. Perhaps that was his form of self-expression – certainly, he does not otherwise seem to have been a particularly communicative child. The guitar, though, became the centre of his world after his parents (who, unlike Jagger's, were not financially comfortable) had bought him his first model when he was fifteen.

It is generally inferred that he was expelled from school for truancy – though this seems to have been one of those mythological stories that cling like barnacles to renegade personalities such as Richard. What seems to have happened is merely that he skipped school early on the last day of term. Any expulsion must therefore have been technical rather than actual (much as footballers can be technically dismissed from the field after the full-time whistle has blown), and in any case it should be noted that the headmaster provided the references which enabled Richard to get a place in art college.

Richard similarly lacked motivation there. He never thought of applying himself to his curricular activities, just as he had never thought of taking up a career, and never concerned himself with considerations of financial security.

So Jagger, Richard and Taylor began playing together that summer, just before Mick went up to the LSE, using Taylor's parents' house as their main rehearsal base where they attempted to pick up the songs of Chuck Berry and other American blues and R&B heroes.

It was not particularly strange that intelligent young men such as those three should have been fascinated by relatively esoteric American music. For one thing, Britain was universally considered a backwater in entertainment terms. Whatever happened in the UK, it was felt, was bound to be a pale shadow of its American counterpart. This received wisdom applied across the entire entertainment spectrum. In the US, the blues were bluesier, the schmaltz was schmaltzier and the pop was poppier. Whether it was Howlin' Wolf or *The Sound Of Music*, it was done better, more authentically across the Atlantic.

But even in the US, rock music had by then lost its sparkle. Little Richard and Jerry Lee Lewis, two performers for whom Jagger readily confessed an early appreciation, had faded from the limelight. Buddy Holly was dead, Elvis Presley was in the army and Chuck Berry was – unavailingly, as it turned out – fighting hard to avoid a prison sentence.

So if even US rock had gone off the boil, it's easy to realise how pitiful British rock was at that time, with derivative performers like Cliff Richard established as the nation's favourite pop star. Even when artists did make a big impact through their work in Britain – such as Gene Vincent and Eddie Cochran – they transpired to be American anyway. (And, by then, Cochran was also dead.).

There were two solitary exceptions to this rule of British rock enfeeblement. The first was Johnny Kidd and the Pirates, who in August 1960 had enjoyed a Number One hit with *Shakin' All Over*, the one genuine British rock classic of pre-Beatle times. Also, there was the one British album for which rock enthusiasts like Keith Richard ever expressed admiration – Billy Fury's debut, *The Sound Of Fury*. He, however, was unable to maintain the standard. British rock otherwise was totally lacking in excitement, imagination, urgency or flair.

All these considerations persuaded many teenagers to look to US R&B and blues for stimulating music – though the final factor was perhaps the most important, which is that such music was then at the heart of an inchoate underground. An interest in R&B was the passport to an exclusive club, where the clientele was an informed and intelligent one.

The music of Chess, whose records carried a distinctive black-and-yellow logo, still fondly remembered to this day, was particularly beguiling. Chess encompassed a range of blues and R&B, with Muddy Waters, Howlin' Wolf, Bo Diddley and Chuck Berry all on their roster. The Rolling Stones were just one of the innumerable groups of that period who congregated round the totem of Chicago music in general and Chess Records in particular.

The musical interests of Brian Jones ran parallel with those of Mick Jagger and Keith Richard, even though his had been fostered in the wholly different environment of Cheltenham, a sedate Regency spa town in Gloucestershire (though one which has in recent times become better known for its wholly insecure security establishment). His full name was Lewis Brian Hopkin-Jones and, like Jagger, he was intellectually bright, gaining nine 'O' and two 'A' levels at Cheltenham Grammar School. His academic abilities and achievements though, were not constructively channelled. He became something of a black sheep, declining to try for the university place that beckoned and that might have allowed him to become what his mother wished (a dentist); and also fathering illegitimate children, an area of production in which his talents were unrivalled.

His wayward behaviour seemed to have been induced by his frustration at being in a place like Cheltenham at all. He was not only highly intelligent, he was also musically gifted, and had mastered several instruments by the time he was in his teens. His mother had taught him piano, and he had sometimes played clarinet and alto sax with local trad jazz bands. His sense of creative asphyxiation, plus the fact that he felt himself isolated from his contemporaries, led him to cast aside the moral code that he had been brought up to believe in.

Since he was passionately interested in blues and R&B, one of the most exciting moments of his adolescence was meeting Alexis Korner, who arrived in Cheltenham on a one-night stand with the Chris Barber Jazz Band. Jones made sure that he introduced himself to such a notable celebrity.

He subsequently spent a year wandering around Scandinavia, leading a kind of Woody Guthrie existence that enabled him to improve his technique as a guitarist. He returned home to the desolate placidity of Cheltenham, briefly joining a local band called The Ramrods and taking employment as a coal-lorry driver. Inevitably, the frustration of his circumstances became unbearable, and he took off for London to look up Alexis Korner.

This presented little difficulty. During their time together, Chris Barber had encouraged Korner to develop an R&B spot of his own within the main performance of the band – which, obviously, consisted entirely of dixieland jazz. Subsequently, Korner was able to leave to start up his own outfit, devoted one hundred per cent to R&B. By the time that Jones made his way to the metropolis, Alexis Korner's Blues Incorporated, featuring the late Cyril Davies on harmonica, had a Saturday evening residency at the Ealing Blues Club in West London. Korner was a generous and approachable man, who viewed his band as a flexible unit, and who was also indefatigable in encouraging youthful talent. Jones renewed his

acquaintance with Korner, and soon found himself making occasional appearances with Blues Incorporated.

Jones' primary objective, though, was to form his own band. To this end, he placed an advertisement in *Jazz News*. He was already playing with Geoff Bradford, another fine blues guitarist, and, in response to the ad, they recruited pianist Ian Stewart, who "looked like a friendly truck driver, with his wide smile and stocky frame" (Barbara Charone: 'Keith Richards'). Although it is not generally appreciated, Stewart has been at the centre of the Stones' circle ever since.

Jagger, Richard and Taylor, meanwhile, had quite independently begun making trips to the Ealing Blues Club – attracted, just as Jones had been, by Korner's fast-growing reputation. Although Jones actually met Jagger and Richard in the Bricklayers' Arms in Broadwick Street, Soho, it was at Ealing that the Jagger-Richard-Taylor axis came into regular contact with the Jones-Bradford-Stewart one as, from the autumn of 1961, they all started making regular weekly pilgrimages to Ealing.

The first occasion on which Jagger and Richard actually stepped up on stage is, inevitably, fondly remembered. With backing provided by members of Korner's team – Davies on harmonica, and a drummer called Charlie Watts – they performed a passable version of *Around And Around*: a Chuck Berry song, naturally.

Jones, who was then referring to himself for professional reasons as Elmo Lewis, was present, along with another aspiring blues singer, P. P. Pond, who later distinguished himself as Paul Jones (no relation), Manfred Mann's lead singer. After his brief appearance, Jagger was encouraged to send Korner a tape of Blue Boys material. Korner, characteristically, reacted kindly, and Jagger was soon making increasingly frequent appearances as one of Blues Incorporated's vocalists. He would perform three numbers, having to share the spoils with Paul Jones and Long John Baldry.

Richard played less regularly, as the group did not really need another guitarist. Even Brian Jones, already better-established in the Korner camp, was surplus to requirements. Blues Incorporated was able to boast a line-up that, retrospectively, is regarded as quite stunning (and even at the time was clearly something special). Apart from those already mentioned, Korner (on guitar), Davies and Watts, the group included Dick Heckstall-Smith (saxophone) and Jack Bruce (bass).

Thus, the nucleus of The Stones began to gather round the paternalistic figure of Korner. Bradford, though, was soon dropped. However excellent as a guitarist, he was a die-hard blues purist, in whose eyes even performers like Berry, Diddley and Jimmy Reed were guilty of commercial opportunism. He found himself at odds with Richard, Jones and Jagger in turn, and soon departed.

This was an ironic turn of events. The fledgling Stones were themselves uncompromisingly sincere about their music, and it was their refusal to countenance compromise that was initially responsible for making them unpopular with fellow musicians and earning them a reputation for bloody-mindedness that stuck to them for years afterwards.

In fact, they simply had ideals about their music – whereas most of the professionals they encountered had long since abandoned theirs in the tedious business of making a living from such a precarious profession. The pros on the club circuit were mostly old sweats, who simply adapted themselves to conform to passing musical fashions. To them, R&B would have been little other than another trend which would pass in six months or so.

Jagger and the others had no respect for such 'professional' practices. They were in the business because they wanted to play a particular kind of music – which was sweaty R&B, as exciting as it was in its home territory of Chicago. They despised music made for commercial convenience, and alienated themselves equally from the troopers on the old pros circuit, and from younger British bands who were simply purveying a debased version of US rock 'n' roll. It is strange to recall now that at that time the Stones positively bristled if they were ever referred to as a rock 'n' roll band. But if The Stones were snobs about their musical tastes, Bradford was a super-snob and didn't fit in. After all, Richard's predilection for Chuck Berry meant that the group was never that far adrift of the commercial mainstream.

Even Blues Incorporated did not conform to the narrow ideological path laid down by The Stones. Their music veered towards jazz and electric blues, and gave little suggestion of the intense and raunchy R&B that the individual members of the still-unformed group were working towards.

The small club scene was just beginning to blossom at that time, in the winter and spring of 1961-2. But R&B blues clubs were still the exception. Trad jazz and skiffle, though fading, remained predominant. Thus, professional opportunities remained few and far between – especially while the band was still completely unknown. Since no-one was interested in booking them, they occasionally attempted to promote their own gigs, a particularly desperate and unpromising course of action.

On Mondays and Wednesdays, Jones, Jagger, Richard and Stewart rehearsed together at the Bricklayer's Arms. Since they couldn't afford to buy records, they had to acquire fresh material any way they could – frequently by calling at the Camden Town flat of Guy Stevens, later a successful record producer, or by making their way to The Cellar, a Kingston-On-Thames club which was one venue where a solid diet of R&B was guaranteed.

By spring 1962 Jagger, Jones and Richard had taken digs together in Edith Grove, off the Fulham Road. Those visitors who saw Edith Grove and lived all reported that the three co-habited in conditions of dreadful squalor. Their circumstances were decidedly impecunious. The weekly rent was invariably paid out of Jagger's academic subsistence grant, and their parents provided occasional financial help – as did Ian Stewart, who at least had a regular job with ICI. His friendship and loyalty was to prove invaluable.

The first real step towards the formation of the group proper occurred on July 12 1962. By then, Blues Incorporated had obtained a residency in the centre of town at the Marquee, then in Oxford Street, on Thursday nights. On that particular July evening, they were booked for a rare BBC radio spot, on Jazz Club. The BBC, however, its financial problems as pressing then as they remain today, stipulated a maximum of six performers – they simply couldn't afford to pay for more. Jagger, still the junior member of the outfit, was the natural candidate for the substitute's bench. Faced with this difficulty, Korner was inclined to refuse the live radio performance, but Jagger insisted; invitations from the BBC were too exceptional to decline. (As it happened, Watts also had to be dropped for the performance, since he was not a member of the Musicians' Union.)

In any case, the occasion represented a great opportunity for Jagger. While Long John Baldry took over Blues Incorporated's residency for the evening, Korner invited Jagger, with his band, to take over the support spot. Thus, The Rolling Stones came into being – taking their name, at Brian Jones' suggestion, from a Muddy Waters song. The 'g' was omitted, in the beginning: The Rollin' Stones.

The group that played that first gig consisted of Jagger (vocals), Jones and Richard (guitars), Stewart (piano), Taylor (bass) and Mick Avory (drums). The latter went on to become a fixture in The Kinks. He was never a regular member of The Stones, he simply helped out on occasions because, like The Beatles, The Stones experienced great problems in finding a suitable drummer. The person who occupied the drum-stool most consistently in their early days was Tony Chapman, though he was only really there because he was the one person the others could get. As a travelling salesman, he generally missed more rehearsals than he attended.

The others were unanimous in wanting Charlie Watts to join, though at this juncture that seemed unlikely. He had a day-job, and shortly was soon to leave Korner simply because Blues Incorporated turned fully pro, and Watts was not anxious to become a full-time professional. (He was replaced in the group by Ginger Baker.)

Nevertheless, after that first date at the Marquee, the group had at last been formed and they started making occasional club appearances during that summer. They did, however, lose the services of Dick Taylor, who decided to take up a place at the Royal College of Art. (He later reappeared as a founder member of The Pretty Things – a group that momentarily scandalised the great British public even more than The Stones.)

Throughout the autumn Brian Jones became increasingly excited about the prospects of making a commercial breakthrough, and gave thought to the image of the group as much as the music it was playing. This did not mean that he was necessarily deserting the musical ideals that had brought The Stones together - merely that he harboured apparently contradictory notions simultaneously.

Certainly, he wanted to accelerate what he envisaged as the group's ineluctable rise to the top by bringing in Carlo Little as drummer. Little had formerly played with Screaming Lord Sutch and the Savages, and was by this time with The Cyril Davies All-Stars, an outfit founded by Davies after he had left Korner to set up his own ethnic R&B group in November 1962. The others, however, demurred, and Little was never invited to join. Somehow they were always waiting for Charlie Watts.

The bass-player's position made vacant by the departure of Dick Taylor was, however, filled. The group was being booked for an increasing number of club dates, and could regularly be caught at the Ealing R&B club, the Marquee, the Red Lion or the Flamingo. In December 1962 they advertised for a bass-player.

Bill Wyman responded, and auditioned for the others at the Wetherby Arms, in the World's End, Chelsea, which The Stones were by now using for rehearsals. Wyman had formerly played alongside Chapman in a South London group called The Cliftons, which had lately disbanded. He was given a job – although the legend surrounding the story (and it's perpetuated not least by Wyman himself) is that it was the size of his amplifier, rather than the quality of his playing, that commended him to the others.

Until he joined The Stones, Wyman had been known as Bill Perks. He deemed his surname an unsuitable one for a budding rock 'n' roll star and changed it accordingly – just as, in early releases, he disguised his actual date of birth to conceal the fact that he was several years older than the others, having been born on October 24, 1936. Something else that was kept from the public in those days was the fact that he had a wife and baby son, Stephen, who'd been born in 1960.

Wyman himself had been born in Lewisham, and educated at Beckenham Grammar School. He had done two years' national service with the RAF in Germany, and by 1962 was doing clerical work for an engineering firm in Streatham. It was a job he retained until he was confident that The Rolling Stones were, financially, a full-time proposition.

At the end of January 1963, the group was finally assembled. After a date The Stones played with Blues By Five, Charlie Watts agreed to defect from one group to the other, and join Jagger and co.

Watts had been born in Islington on June 2 1941, and had gone to art school in Harrow. After completing his course he joined an advertising agency and was employed there, doing lettering as a commercial artist,

when he first threw in his lot with The Stones. As a jazz musician, his background in music could be said to have been more serious than that of the others. He'd always believed that work came first, however, which is why he initially declined invitations to join The Stones (after Ian Stewart had originally recommended him, he'd had several opportunities to join), and also why he'd refused to go fully-pro with Alexis Korner, and instead played with Blues By Five (or, as occasion demanded, Blues By Six), which was a Korner offshoot band that Brian Jones had formerly been involved with.

Buoyant with expectation now that the group was a six-man team, and a complete self-sufficient line-up at last, The Rolling Stones went into IBC recording studios in Portland Place, with a close friend, studio engineer (and now producer) Glyn Johns. It was their first recording experience, and in one afternoon they cut five songs, all R&B standards: *I Want To Be Loved*, *Roadrunner*, *Diddley Diddley Daddy*, *Honey, What's Wrong* and *Bright Lights, Big City*. Naturally, the completed tapes were despatched at the earliest opportunity to a number of record companies. None showed the slightest interest.

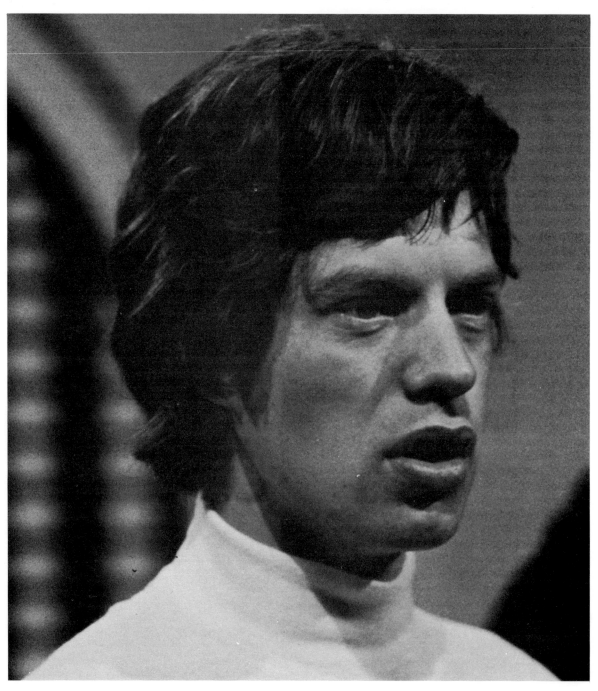

2

Mick Jagger could have gone into plastics, computers, into journalism or the law; he could have designed hovercraft or joined a grocery chain: whatever he had chosen to do, he would undoubtedly have distinguished himself in his chosen field. He was that kind of super-confident and well-motivated career type; a scion of a disciplined lower-middle-class household; a high achiever.

Presumably, he happened to achieve what he did in the field of music simply because he was opportunely placed at a convenient time – when the whole pattern of popular music was undergoing fundamental change and, under the impact of The Beatles, the balance of power was shifting from America to Britain. He had abilities combined with the kind of assertive character that understood how to use them to their maximum; but he was also in the right place at the right time.

His parents were concerned about his interest in music – though, typically, they were supportive rather than censorious, and they paid for some of The Stones' early equipment. Jagger in turn remained the dutiful son and, for all the snowballing interest in the group, stuck to his studies at the LSE. While Richard and Jones rehearsed hard all day at Edith Grove, playing Jimmy Reed material *ad infinitum*, and even Watts sometimes stayed there, Stewart and Wyman stayed in the nine-to-five routine, and Jagger pursued his degree course.

The Stones were already becoming notorious on the London club circuit and a vicious circle was being created. They were highly defensive about their own areas of musical interest and tended to treat those who gave the appearance of being career musicians with some scorn. As other musicians became wary, so The Stones kept their own counsel. The old pros came to resent their stand-offishness and air of apparent arrogance – so The Stones withdrew further, deliberately detaching themselves from the boozy companionship of the others on the club circuit. And so on. Social barriers were erected, The Stones became a group apart. They formed a tight circle which outsiders rarely penetrated.

Strangely, this situation has persisted throughout. Apart from one or two isolated occasions, The Stones have never hobnobbed with their peers on the rock circuit.

Surprising as it seems in retrospect, the group was deeply wounded by the lack of response generated by the tapes from the IBC studios. They regarded it as a considerable setback. It was clear that what they needed was a launching-pad.

It was Giorgio Gomelsky who provided one for them. He was the founder/manager of an R&B club that

operated from within the Station Hotel in Kew Road, Richmond. In January 1963 his resident group, the Dave Hunt R&B Band missed one gig too many (Hunt had always had trouble keeping the line-up together) and Gomelsky decided to dispense with their services. The Stones, and Brian Jones in particular, had already been making regular overtures to him, and so he phoned up Ian Stewart and offered them the weekly engagement.

Gomelsky, a keen jazz fan of Russian descent, had previously tried his hand at experimental film-making, and had originally arrived in Richmond in 1960 to make a film about Chris Barber at the 1st National Jazz Festival, held at the athletic ground in the Old Deer Park. Gomelsky took a hand in organising future events – which, at his suggestion, became Jazz *and Blues* festivals – and also started his own R&B club.

The Stones always admitted that it wasn't until they began their Richmond residency that they got going. In a sense, it was their Star Club, Hamburg – for it was at Richmond that they honed their style, consolidated their repertoire and were able to charm and excite their audiences. There was little response at first – people just stood and watched them – but then one or two started dancing on the tables (the only furniture the club possessed) towards the climax of The Stones' act, and quickly the audiences went wild. The atmosphere generated in that small back room of a nondescript pub (which, despite its grandsounding name, is all that the Station Hotel was) must have been fantastic. Every Sunday would have been a red-letter day for teenagers living in those parts of West London.

The audience barely approached fifty for The Stones' first date there in February (when the evening's takings amounted to seven pounds ten shillings), but by the beginning of April there were over three hundred and fifty packed in, many of whom had queued for some time for the privilege. It was because of the special success of The Stones that Gomelsky realised that he should actually have a proper name for his club. So he called it The Crawdaddy, taking the title from a Bo Diddley dance number that was frequently the closing highlight of The Stones' performance.

By this point, The Stones were still barely scratching a living, and in the early months of 1963 were only making what they received from The Crawdaddy. Within a short time, they had taken on a second Sunday residency, playing in the afternoons at Ken Colyer's Studio 51 in Great Newport Street, just off Charing Cross Road.

On April 13, 1963, the *Richmond & Twickenham Times* provided The Stones with their first genuine press notice. A highly encouraging one it was, too – not solely because of its unbridled enthusiasm for The Stones themselves, but also because it emphasized the fast-growing popularity of R&B, which was just beginning to elbow jazz aside. Modern jazz had never commanded a wide audience anyway, and trad was, like skiffle before it, clearly in decline. It was with the breakthrough of groups like The Stones, of course, that the replacement of jazz by R&B as the staple fare of most small clubs was accelerated. In fact, the arrival of The Stones at Studio 51 signalled that Ken Colyer's club was in the process of making that very transition.

While they were at The Crawdaddy, Gomelsky looked after the group and attended to their interests. If one wants to draw further parallels with The Beatles' story, then he was their Allan Williams – their unofficial, and certainly unpaid, manager. He tried to arouse interest in the IBC tape, for example, though once more without success.

By Easter there were long queues outside the club whenever The Stones were due to make an appearance (they were, at one stage, playing there four evenings a week). Eric Clapton and other members of the as-yet unformed Yardbirds were among those who went regularly. Of those from outside the immediate locality who had been tipped off to see them were The Beatles, who managed to squeeze in on April 21, 1963 and catch the last twenty minutes of their act. George Harrison was particularly impressed. He actually recommended the group to Dick Rowe, the A&R manager at Decca who was never allowed to forget that he had turned down The Beatles; Harrison, at least, gave him the opportunity of almost compensating for the most famous *faux pas* in the history of popular music.

However, the train of events that led to The Stones' breakthrough actually started elsewhere. Gomelsky invited a freelance journalist, Peter Jones, down to the club to see his group. Jones was thoroughly impressed. He then contacted Norman Jopling, a staff writer on *Record Mirror*, who made it along to the Crawdaddy, and duly gave The Rolling Stones what proved to be their first publicity in a national newspaper.

That piece would probably have alerted many to the existence of the band. Even before it appeared, however, Jones had also contacted a young publicist, Andrew Oldham, who had done some work for Brian Epstein and The Beatles earlier in the year, telling him that Jopling was about to file an ecstatic review of the group.

Oldham was electrified when he saw The Rolling Stones in performance. The joint really was jumping – and probably it was the fervour of the fans gathered there, as much as the musical strengths of the group itself, that told Oldham that he was on to something big. Obviously, the crowd consisted of *bona fide* R&B fanatics who loved the music – but over and above that it was clear that The Stones had a definite visual appeal; the band itself had personality, and style. For all that the group seemed to appeal predominantly to the males in the audience (so, at the beginning, did The Beatles), and

that the feminine reaction to them was less certain, Oldham sensed that the group had an exciting presence, and a sexuality which had a potentially unlimited appeal.

No doubt the next few days were desperately anxious ones for Oldham. By this time, The Beatles were flying high – *From Me To You* was at the top of the charts – and agents were already scouring the country (Liverpool in particular) for groups most likely to succeed.

There was little that Oldham could do on his own, but he persuaded Eric Easton to return to The Crawdaddy with him to see The Stones. Easton was a fifty-year-old one-time mill-owner from the North who had become a successful show-business agent. He had offices in Regent Street, and Oldham rented space from him to run his freelance publicity business.

Easton endorsed Oldham's opinion of the group, and after that things moved speedily. The chase for young talent was so hot that both felt there was not a minute to lose. They signed The Rolling Stones to a management deal, which was agreed at the Wetherby Arms. Neither were Oldham and Easton merely co-managers; there was a clause in the contract which stipulated that they were to supervise The Stones' recording sessions, and that a recording company's own A&R men would be unable to interfere.

This was a most unusual agreement, and apparently demonstrated that The Stones had fallen hook, line and sinker for Oldham's persuasive patter. Indeed, it seems to have been his blithe assurances that he was familiar with the fine points of recording technique that persuaded The Stones to sign with him and abandon Gomelsky.

Oldham, of course, was bluffing. He'd never been allowed to turn the light on in a recording studio, let alone fiddle with more important knobs and switches. It would, however, have been hard to pull the wool over Jagger's eyes. Perhaps the latter reasoned that, even if Oldham wasn't telling the truth, he was so earnestly convincing that he would be bound to make a good manager.

Gomelsky was thus left behind at Richmond. He was deprived, in turn, of both his protégés and his club. For once Oldham had taken charge, and Fleet Street had begun to depict The Stones as an unsavoury modern phenomenon, the brewery which owned the Station Hotel became alarmed, and turfed out The Crawdaddy – though Gomelsky soon found alternative premises at the athletic ground. He also soon discovered another group that was almost capable of filling The Stones' shoes: The Yardbirds. That time he didn't lose out, and it was as manager and producer of them that he achieved a measure of personal fame.

Having signed The Stones, Oldham straightaway secured them a recording contract with Decca. Some months earlier this would have been a major achievement on his part. By May 1963, however, The Beatles had thrown the industry into a ferment, and all

companies were eagerly and indiscriminately snapping up groups. In addition Rowe, as was noted earlier, was trying to live down his gigantic personal blunder. Oldham's task was made even easier, of course, by the fact that George Harrison had already alerted Rowe to the qualities of The Stones. In fact, the tide was running so strongly in favour of promising bands that Oldham was even able to secure The Stones a generous royalty rate (something The Beatles certainly didn't enjoy at EMI).

Oldham's next action was less welcome. He dropped Ian Stewart from the line-up, telling him quite bluntly that his straight image conflicted with the one he wanted the group to project. Poor Stewart was given subservient duties as a road manager.

The matter illustrated two points: firstly that Oldham, although only nineteen, was conducting his business with the group with total confidence, and he must have felt very sure of his ground to have acted so decisively so swiftly.

What was also apparent was that Oldham actually had a pre-conceived idea of the type of group he wanted The Stones to be. In this respect, Stewart's failing was probably less that he looked conventional in appearance than that he always looked *friendly*: that undoubtedly conflicted with Oldham's designs for the group.

So why did The Stones accept the sudden banishment of one of their founder-members so meekly? One can only conjecture, but they must have had total faith in Oldham and they must, as a group, have wanted very much to succeed. The incident is certainly an unpleasant one in the history of The Stones, and it invites another parallel with The Beatles – the sacking of Pete Best. Whereas the public retrospectively held The Beatles to account for their action there, the abrupt dismissal of Ian Stewart has never been held against The Stones. In this respect, The Stones have hitherto been let off lightly. The group is said to have regretted it since, agreeing that the whole episode was badly handled. Those who argue that Pete Best got the rougher deal, because he was cast entirely aside whereas Stewart has at least remained in The Stones' camp ever since should remember that Best was sacked on grounds that virtually amounted to professional incompetence; Stewart's services were dispensed with because Oldham didn't like the way he looked. No-one ever suggested that there was anything wrong with his professional abilities.

It's interesting to speculate why Stewart has never been re-admitted to the group in the years since, once The Stones' image had been immutably fixed anyway. A possible answer is that The Stones successfully kept the whole thing so quiet for so long that by the time it became public knowledge it would not have been easy to re-admit him. The group would effectively have been confirming that it was an injustice ever to have relegated him.

So the six became five – and, had Brian Jones had his way, the five would have become four. He wanted the others to drop Mick Jagger so that he could handle lead vocals himself. Sounds ludicrous, doesn't it? Well, Jones' attempts at self-promotion were not very successful – though at the time it seemed that he tried to persuade Eric Easton that Jagger was not a good enough singer. Easton seems to have come close to endorsing his opinion, especially after the group had failed an early audition for the BBC Radio show, *Saturday Club*, since presenter Brian Matthews also disliked Jagger's singing. In the end, of course, Jones got nowhere; he merely stored up resentment against himself. The others may have consented to drop Stewart – but it was inconceivable that they would have countenanced the sacking of Jagger.

The Rolling Stones' first recording session proper took place on May 10 1963 in Olympic Sound studios. The basic problem, for a group which had not then considered writing its own material, was – what should they record? Obviously, it had to be commercial – Oldham would have insisted on that, and so would Decca – and the group instinctively concurred, anyway. Nevertheless, they clearly didn't want to record anything that compromised them from the outset.

In the end, the choice neatly reconciled such disparate objectives. Inevitably, it was a Chuck Berry song, though *Come On* had the great advantage of never having been issued in this country (Jagger had bought it as an import single) and it was thus unlikely either that the potential audience would ever have heard it before, or that any other group would also cover it. For a B-side they recorded Willie Dixon's *I Want To Be Loved* (one of the songs they had featured on the IBC tape), which included a harmonica solo from Jones.

Oldham was in charge of the session – though he, of course, was as raw a newcomer to recording studios as the others. It is not, perhaps, surprising that Decca immediately rejected the proffered tapes as of sub-standard quality, and sent the group into the company's own West Hampstead studios to do it all over again. The results, second time, were more satisfactory, and the record was released on June 7 1963.

There have been better debut singles, but *Come On* certainly served its purpose of drawing attention to the group. The recording had a rare sense of urgency, and showed an awareness of grabbing the listener's attention with the opening bars. There was also a powerful vocal from Jagger.

The song began to receive radio air-play, and shortly after its release The Rolling Stones made their television debut, performing both sides of the single on *Thank Your Lucky Stars*. Such early appearances were made particularly memorable by the fact that Oldham had persuaded them all to don similar garb – houndstooth check jackets with velvet half-collars, white shirt, dark tie, black trousers and Chelsea boots. As an early example of Carnaby Street chic, the ensemble was interesting, and perhaps even valuable; as a serious uniform for The Rolling Stones it was risible. They had discarded it within months, but, even allowing for the sartorial standards of the time, it was amazing that Oldham ever persuaded them into the gear in the first place.

Keith Richard has sometimes suggested that the fact that Oldham put them all into matching clothes – in the manner of The Beatles – proves that far from creating their image, Oldham had actually wished to clean up the image that the group had already established for themselves. However, there is overwhelming evidence to refute this. Obviously, Oldham all along took what The Beatles were doing as his criterion, and he seems to have had in mind from the start the notion of emphasising the contrasts between Epstein's group and his own. However, both he and The Stones probably wanted to tread warily at the very beginning – hence, the houndstooth jackets.

As it happened, the fact that they were all turned out so neatly hardly created a favourable impression with the nation's viewers anyway. From the outset, The Stones generated a hostile audience reaction. It's difficult to explain now why it should have been so. Partly, it was their long hair. Clearly, The Beatles had reached the boundaries of what was acceptable – and The Stones had gone way beyond them. Even so, their hair, unremarkable by today's standards, was merely shaggy and somewhat unkempt. It was not, of course, dirty, although the average Englishman, of average prejudices, immediately numbered the five among the nation's great unwashed.

Even more than their appearance, however, their manner was calculated to affront a nationwide audience. As led by Jagger, the group came across as surly, sneering and deliberately provocative. It was an act meant to achieve a particular response from the audience to generate maximum publicity. It did so.

With the national press already beginning to turn its attention towards them – and Stone-bashing was shortly to become a stock-in-trade of Fleet Street's popular dailies – the group was obviously making an impression, and in July 1963 Come On entered the charts.

That moment, finally, was the watershed. Wyman gave in his notice to the Streatham engineering company, and Jagger, having completed exactly two years of his course, decided to quit academic life. "We all got busier and busier," he later remembered, "until we made the record. Then when that got into the charts, things became really hectic, and got to such a state that I decided to leave the LSE."

"My tutors were very decent about it, and they told me I could return after a year if things didn't work out. So, my options were open. That's the best way to have things." Finally, The Stones had become a full-time group.

Young as he was, Andrew Oldham definitely had visions of becoming as celebrated a manager as Brian Epstein. It was a corollary of this that he wanted to put The Stones on a plateau alongside The Beatles. To this end, he deliberately presented The Stones as the antithesis of The Beatles. Epstein wanted his group to seem pure, smart and innocuous. Fair enough then, Oldham would display his as dirty, uncouth and dangerous. As a promotional technique it worked only too effectively. The Beatles became the kids who charmed a nation; The Stones were the louts who kicked it in the bollocks. Almost from the very start of their recording career, Jagger and co. received more national press coverage than any group except The Beatles. The maxim that "all publicity is good publicity" had been around for some time and Oldham made it ring more resoundingly true than ever.

However, it would be a mistake to exaggerate the speed of the ascent of The Stones. During 1963, The Beatles carried all before them and Merseybeat was the dominant sound of the time. An increasing number were intrigued by The Stones – but it would be a fallacy to suggest that they commanded anything like a wide audience. During the summer they continued playing club dates, and carried on with their Sunday afternoon residency at Studio 51 (and still used it as their rehearsal base). After the limited success of Come On they did begin to undertake ballroom dates – Middlesbro' on August 5 was the first one. On August 11 they returned to familiar terrain when they appeared back in Richmond, towards the bottom of the bill at the annual Jazz and Blues Festival.

They also recorded a follow-up single at this time – the Coasters' Poison Ivy, backed with their version of Fortune Teller. In fact, no-one was very satisfied with the results. Also, Come On, though it never rose very high in the charts (it lodged just outside the Top 20) did demonstrate unusual staying-power. So, while it was still in the charts, there was little point in releasing a follow-up – especially one about which all concerned harboured doubts. At the last minute, the release of Poison Ivy was cancelled.

On September 29, The Rolling Stones embarked on their first countrywide theatre tour. They were booked on to a bill that was headlined by the Everly Brothers and Bo Diddley, who was making his UK concert debut. Sixty dates were scheduled over a thirty-day period but though the bill seemed attractive enough, ticket sales were disappointing, and before the end of the first week, promoter Don Arden had to fly in Little Richard to boost the box-office appeal of the package.

Naturally, The Stones were delighted to find themselves on the same bill as Bo Diddley. "He's one of our big influences," enthused Jagger, for the benefit of anyone who hadn't understood that already. He immediately sensed that discretion was the better part of valour, and announced that the group would be dropping all Bo Diddley numbers from their repertoire for the tour.

Eager to learn, The Stones socialised with Diddley and his entourage. The fraternisation had several

An early appearance on *Ready, Steady, Go.*

advantages – Jerome Green taught Jagger much about playing maraccas; the group learned about American instruments and amplification equipment, which at that time were greatly superior to anything that was readily available in Britain; and Jones, Watts and Wyman actually supported Bo when he made a live appearance on the BBC's Saturday Club. (By this time, The Stones themselves had appeared on the programme).

Carefully nursed by an indefatigable Oldham, The Stones' reputation continued to grow. Despite the handicap of arriving on the scene after The Beatles *et al*, the group gradually managed to assert its individuality and become fixed in the public imagination. As a vocalist, Jagger always gave the public full measure, taking advantage of the fact that his movements were not impeded by the necessity of playing an instrument to cavort freely and effectively round the microphone. At times, he'd clap his hands by the side of his head – a movement which became a Jagger trademark.

He became one of the great performers in rock, and virtually established the ground-rules for how a vocalist should disport himself on stage, to the extent that virtually every rock vocalist ever since has seemed guilty, to some degree, of plagiarism. (The ones who, after Jagger, managed to establish their own distinctive styles – Joe Cocker, for example – can be counted on the fingers of one hand.)

Meanwhile, and in direct contrast to Jagger's exuberant antics, the group itself helped to popularise a dance called the Nod, which involved a minimum of movement or exertion. In a strange way, this represented the beginning of the riposte of the metropolis to the pre-eminence achieved by Liverpool; the Nod was the first aspect of pop music, post-Beatle, that was entirely Southern-based and had nothing to do with the North. The dance was relaxed and cool, and can be seen as one of the early elements that coalesced into the mod sub-culture.

Finally, The Stones had their own word – nankies – for those little men who thought they represented high and mighty authority; The Stones encountered them quite a lot. They even had a contemptuous nankie facial expression, which was obtained by pulling down the skin under the eyes and pushing the nostrils upwards. You think I'm joking? There are photographs to prove it; Jones and Richard seem to have been especially proficient at nankering.

However bizarre these characteristics, they all helped to provide The Stones with a distinct identity at a moment when record companies were producing new groups weekly. It was *Ready, Steady, Go!* that helped to cement an awareness of The Stones in the minds of the adolescent generation. The group made several appearances, and proved extremely popular guests on the programme.

While touring with the Everly/Diddley package, The Stones all called in at the Cavern in Liverpool, to see what it was actually like and to hear the Big Three live on stage. They were given a warm reception by the

audience – a measure of how their standing had improved as a result of *Ready, Steady, Go!* appearances. As a result of their visit, they were prevailed upon to return as artists and perform there themselves.

It was also in Liverpool, while staying in one of the city's hotels, that the group members suddenly discovered that Brian Jones was collecting five pounds more a week in wages than the others, on the basis that he was the group leader.

The others were flabbergasted. Jones hadn't managed to oust Jagger, but he had arrived at this secret agreement with Eric Easton. Needless to say, the basis for any such arrangement was entirely spurious, even apart from the fact that he had seriously deceived his colleagues.

In a sense, the Jones-Jagger personality war had been simmering throughout the year. Jones considered himself the rightful leader of the band, but whatever authority he had was increasingly undermined by the stronger personality of Jagger.

Jones' behaviour was understandable only in so far as he had been the recognised leader at the beginning – Jagger indeed had consciously tried *not* to assert himself as the dominant personality. Furthermore, it was actually necessary for Jones (in his own opinion) to be leader. As Keith Richard explained, "Brian had this obsession about success. We all remembered him after a Beatles' concert at the Royal Albert Hall. He'd gone backstage and been mistaken for someone connected with the group. He therefore became the object of frenzied, teenage adulation. He loved it, and desperately craved more." Believe it or not, Jones still harboured a parellel obsession, which was to communicate the blues to the British public. It was a contradiction that has been noted earlier. In Jones' defence it should be pointed out that although today it is realised that the two aims were irreconcilable, at the time, such was the volatile atmosphere, anything seemed possible.

So, Jones was not a pleasant personality. He was always jealous of everyone, and he became increasingly more jealous as he receded into the background. He was popular with the fans, but Jagger was unarguably recognised as the front-man. (Especially once the group started making frequent television appearances; television producers rarely allow the cameras to focus on anyone other than the vocalist.)

Two other developments further weakened Jones' position within the group. The first is that Jagger and Richard had by now moved out of Edith Grove into new accomodation, which they shared with Oldham. As the three became increasingly adept at manipulating the media, so the attention shifted firmly to Jagger and Richard, whom the press painted black. (The problem for Jones was that he occasionally looked angelic so that, even though those filing paternity suits knew differently, he did not appear to fit the myths the press were creating.) Secondly, of course, once the group had appreciated how essential it was to come up with their own material, then the two became even more of a focal point; Jones' profile receded several more notches.

Jones' main problem, however, was simply the emergence of Jagger as the dominant personality within the group. He was the natural leader – and Jones couldn't cope with that. From the day in the Liverpool hotel when the others found out how he had been deceiving them, he became more mistrusted and less influential.

"That," said Richard, "was the beginning of the end for Jones."

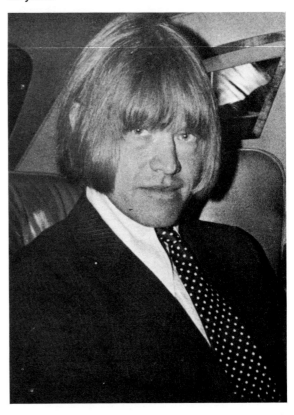

Brian Jones on his way to trial.

3

With the increasing ostracism of Jones, Jagger became an ever more dominant personality within the group. He didn't actively seek the status of group leader – it just fell naturally to him, partly because he was the strongest and most articulate personality and partly because he, as vocalist, was the one on whom the media concentrated. Jagger, though, was still feeling his way, and it was Keith who first found his feet in the recording studio, and became the more decisive influence there.

To begin with, however, the band was hesitant and uncertain at recording sessions. There is nothing particularly surprising in this. After all, most contemporary musicians would have been nonplussed by the technicalities of the studio; sessions were routinely handled by experienced record company employees. There were virtually no independent producers, and musicians would not have been capable of producing their own work. The Stones would have been especially at sea. After all, The Beatles had the services of George Martin, even then one of the best producers in the business; whereas, under the terms of their contract, The Stones' sessions were supervised by Oldham – and he, like them, was a novice in such matters.

It would be nice to be able to say that what they all lacked in expertise they made up for in dynamic energy, an instinctive appreciation of recording methods and a positive sense of direction. But this would not be true: they did not really know what they wanted – not at first – and finding out took some time. Decca was certainly not impressed by the early efforts, and the delay between the release of the first and the second Stones single can be attributed partly to their insistence on the achievement of a satisfactory recording standard (they had after all rejected *Poison Ivy*, the title slated for single release that summer) and partly to the fact that The Stones themselves were unsure about the kind of follow-up they wanted to put out. Leadership, whether from Jagger or anyone else, was demonstrably absent at this juncture.

Thus the group had thrashed around inconclusively. Jagger and Richard had even tried to compose a song together, but the results were unsatisfactory and that avenue was, for the time being, left unexplored. What was needed was a kind of compromise between the unapologetically commercial approach which logic dictated, and the R&B/blues sound on which they had moulded their own, somewhat elitist, image. The most inviting compromise was inevitably a Chuck Berry number, but they'd adopted that course the last time. Something different was now required.

The problem was solved for them by Andrew Oldham. One Sunday in early November, while walking in Jermyn Street, in London's Piccadilly area, he literally bumped into John Lennon and Paul McCartney, who had just attended a lunch at the Savoy Hotel for the Variety Club of Great Britain. Oldham knew them well – after all, he had been briefly engaged to look after the Beatles' publicity at the beginning of the year. During the course of their conversation, Oldham mentioned the difficulties The Stones were experiencing in finding a suitable song for their second single. "Now, there's a funny thing," said John (or words to that effect), "we just happened to be composing a new one when you came along. . . ."

At that time, of course, The Beatles were indeed composing new songs continuously to meet an ever-rising demand – both to keep pace with their own heavy recording schedule and also to supply at least some of the countless requests for material from other artists. Everyone wanted to get on the bandwagon – a feeling engendered partly by opportunism, of course, but also partly by a sense of realism: under the auspices of Brian Epstein and The Beatles, Merseybeat had carried all before it during the year, and it seemed as though nothing was assured of success unless it bore its stamp.

Lennon and McCartney readily agreed to accompany Oldham to Studio 51 where The Stones were rehearsing. Naturally, the Stones professed great interest in the song The Beatles were working on; *I Wanna Be Your Man* was finished there and then. Unlike much of the other material which Lennon and McCartney wrote to order, this wasn't a song which The Beatles gave away and then disregarded themselves – it was included on *With The Beatles* with a vocal from Ringo; but by the time the album came out, The Stones' version was already in the charts.

The Stones learned the song straightaway, and recorded it a fortnight later in Kingsway studios, with Easton at the production controls in place of Oldham, who was absent in France. They had tried to interpret the song in their own style, to make it distinctively theirs rather than just another Lennon-McCartney cover. By comparing their version with The Beatles' own it is clear that whereas The Beatles' is rather happy-go-lucky, theirs is almost threatening, with Jagger beginning to develop his leering vocal style. It was a distinction which epitomised the vast gulf in the public personae of the groups themselves.

Nevertheless, the mere fact that they found it necessary to seek assistance of The Beatles rankled. After all, The Stones had to survive for long enough in their giant shadow, and during their first heady months of fame especially, the attention of both the music business itself and the public was so single-mindedly fixed on The Beatles that other acts could exist only in relation to them, as though The Beatles were at the centre of the firmament, with everything else spinning around them.

. There was the added problem for The Stones that they were obsessed with making it on their own terms, and not compromising their R&B ideals – and The Beatles, for all the affection in which the UK public held them, were still reckoned to be operating strictly within the traditional framework of popular music.

In the end, however, without too many qualms of conscience, The Stones shelved their desperate concern to make an individual impact in order to snatch at this ready-made chance of commercial success; they weren't about to look a gift-horse in the mouth.

It was noticeable though, that the group – and Jagger in particular – deeply resented suggestions that they owed their commercial breakthrough to The Beatles. Jagger's comments on the single emphasised the facts that (a) The Stones had given it a distinctive treatment of their own; (b) they had changed it still further for live performances and (c) it was never one of the group's own favourite singles anyway.

The B-side was a Stones' original – their first, although *Stoned* could hardly be dignified with the word 'composition'. It was just a bluesy instrumental, featuring Ian Stewart on keyboards, punctuated by interjections from Jagger, and somewhat reminiscent of the one song guaranteed to fill the dance-floor at all the clubs, Booker T. & the M.G.s' *Green Onions. Stoned* had a more gentle rhythm, however, and seemed custom-made for energy-conserving dance. It was touted as "being perfect for Nod dancers".

For this first piece of original work, Jagger and Richard dubbed themselves Nanker & Phelge, pseudonyms they retained for a little while. 'Nanker' was used as a result of their fascination with 'nankering', and (Jimmy) Phelge was – apparently – a printer who had once shared their communal squalor at Edith Grove.

Of course, *I Wanna Be Your Man* was successful, and it lodged for some time just outside the Top 10. Not a runaway hit, therefore, but it generated sufficient interest to show that the Stones were continuing to build on their base of popular appeal.

They were duly voted the sixth most popular UK group in the New Musical Express poll at the end of the year – behind the Beatles, the Searchers, Gerry & the Pacemakers, the Shadows and the Springfields, but ahead of everybody else. It was an encouraging result for a band which hadn't yet cracked the Top Ten, and demonstrated that from the start The Stones had a powerful charisma. Their support may have been relatively narrow-based (and this point will be discussed in greater detail later), but it was fervently loyal.

Nineteen sixty-three had been an incredible year: the year of the Profumo scandal in the UK and the assassination of President Kennedy in the US. In the UK, The Beatles had been barely-known outside Liverpool at the start of the year, and by the end of it they were demi-gods; for The Stones, barely-known anywhere back then, the year had begun with a scramble to obtain the Richmond residency and had concluded with their being placed sixth in a nationwide poll. It was progress that was more steady than heady, but was nonetheless commendable for all that.

Nevertheless, at this stage – despite the reasonable level of success and Oldham's inchoate image-making, there was still an engaging ingenuousness about The Stones.

It's noticeable that, just as Jagger had displayed great shrewdness in deciding when to abandon his LSE course, so he was all the time hedging his bets – "keeping my options open", as he put it – and tempering the group's in-built waywardness with a cool appreciation of the realities of the business. "We still have the enthusiasm to treat the business as an enjoyable pastime," he told one reporter, "but also the professionalism to realise that you can't turn up late for dates and that sort of thing."

This is a path which Jagger has followed unswervingly ever since. The quote is illuminating, however, because he has hardly been as frank about his deliberately calculated attitudes ever since – or, come to that, as deferential and obliging to reporters.

Those were indeed early days. The Stones were then noviates in the great and glamorous world of show business – and they still tingled with excitement when rubbing shoulders with the famous names. Especially top American stars. A meeting with Gene Pitney went off particularly harmoniously.

The group met him in early December 1963 during rehearsals for Thank Your Lucky Stars. "We watched him rehearse and were all knocked out because he was so professional," enthused Jagger. "And talking to him about records we were impressed at his knowledge of the backroom scenes in recording." A mutual admiration society quickly developed. Pitney thought The Stones "a great bunch of lads", even though he also observed that they "looked a wild crew, with all that long hair.".

The friendship certainly seemed a result of the attraction of opposites, even apart from the fact that Pitney and the Rolling Stones occupied opposite extremes of the tonsorial spectrum. Pitney, as well as always appearing freshly-barbered, was invariably conservatively-dressed, while The Stones' appearance, demeanour and attitudes all inclined towards the radical. They'd been introduced by Oldham – he was Pitney's publicist too – and so convivial was the relationship that Jagger and Richard presented Pitney with a song of their own.

With Oldham, Jagger and Richard rooming together in Willesden, Oldham had had an opportunity to impress on the others the inestimable value of composing their own material. Mick and Keith had

Gene Pitney.

hardly believed it was within their capabilities to do that: only Americans and Lennon-McCartney composed songs. Oldham, however, determined that his protégés should emulate the Beatles in every possible respect, insisted.

Jagger and Richard's first efforts together, like Lennon-McCartney's earliest collaborations, were rather gauche. In fact, they were constructed entirely along conventional lines, with romantic lyrics. 'Slushy beat ballads' might have been an apposite description of material like *It Should Be You*, which was actually a song that had been considered for the group's second single. They had recorded it, but it had not been thought strong enough, and it was passed over to another artiste on Decca's books, George Bean, who recorded that and another Jagger-Richard song, *Will You Be My Lover Tonight* on a single produced by Andrew Oldham. The record flopped. The only reason to pluck Bean's name from the obscurity of history is that he was the very first performer to cover original Rolling Stones' material.

Gene Pitney was the second. He suggested modifications in the song The Stones had proffered, so that it suited the lachrymose style he had made his own. Thus the song became *That Girl Belongs To Yesterday*, and it reached the Top 10 the following year.

Now Pitney was an international star, and could have called upon the songwriting services of any number of acclaimed teams. (Burt Bacharach and Hal David; Barry

Mann and Cynthia Weil; Randy Newman – all composed some of his other hits), but he gratefully accepted the opportunity to record something by this fledgling duo.

Putting himself in the hands of of a British songwriting team was a useful means of consolidating his position in the UK market where, in contrast to achievements elsewhere, he had previously scored only one major hit, *Twenty-Four Hours From Tulsa*. It also made him considerably more acceptable to the new, post-Beatle audience. Other recording stars of the early sixties, Bobby Vee, for example, lost their footing completely in the Beatles landslide; Pitney was able to turn events to his advantage.

For The Stones, it was a unique opportunity to work with someone who had already achieved the kind of commercial success for which they yearned. In the event, *That Girl Belongs To Yesterday* did benefit both parties: Pitney advanced his cause in the UK, while The Stones' advanced theirs in the US, where Pitney's name was enough to take it into the charts. In addition, the song was the first Jagger-Richard composition to reach the UK Top Ten.

Even apart from these strictly self-interested considerations however, the acts had tangible reasons for wanting to work with one another. They each respected the other's work, and they also seemed to hit it off socially. At the time, it seemed an exciting development in the career of the Rolling Stones; twenty years on, it seems one of the more bizarre episodes of their story. Probably this is because Pitney sacrificed his artistry to his style in the cause of continuous chart success, and then allowed his career to deteriorate entirely in the later sixties. At the time he encountered the Stones, he had more to commend him than just a prestigious name; he was young, enterprising, resourceful, creative and, unlike the majority of his contemporaries, was *au fait* with recording technique. For some time to come, he remained a close associate of The Stones.

The group themselves were soon making much more valuable contacts. In January 1964 they were booked for their second UK tour. Johnny Kidd and the Pirates and Marty Wilde were subsidiary attractions. The Stones were joint bill-toppers along with the Ronettes, one of producer Phil Spector's groups who'd just had great success in October 1963 with *Be My Baby*.

While the tour itself was an immense success – with 'house full' notices everywhere the package appeared and, more importantly perhaps, a genuinely enthusiastic audience response wherever they played – its star attractions were getting on famously. The Stones were enamoured of the girls, feeling that they sounded equally as good on stage as on their records (which, given the elaborate and distinctive production on their singles, was no small achievement), while the Ronettes found much to admire in The Stones. "I think the boys could be really big in the States," enthused Estelle Bennett, one of the three members of the vocal group, "what with their special brand of music and everything. And their suits, and they way they grow their hair – they're great."

What even the tour promoters – the George Cooper Organisation – could hardly have foreseen was how well the two acts would complement one another. First of all, they adopted a similarly natural style of stage presentation. As Phil Spector said, "My girls did not just stand there wearing fairy-tale dresses and praying to their hearts when the word 'heart' came around. And the Rolling Stones were the same, always natural."

The Ronettes had thrown over conventional stage presentations in favour of an approach that was more in tune with those increasingly permissive times – one which emphasised their basic sexuality. In this way, too, The Stones had an equivalent appeal – or at least Jagger did. "Mick was such a good mover," remembers group leader Ronnie Spector, "that the girls all took to him. He was so sexy, provocative and gorgeous onstage." Of all the reasons for the group's success, this is the one most frequently overlooked. Jagger did have great presence in live performance, and was able to convey great sexual charm, even when not trying particularly hard to do so – as that time it was still Jones who tried most deliberately to provoke the female contingent in the audience. Jagger's own performance was not then noted for its athleticism. He tended to stand still and try to achieve a distinctive presence by means of hand gestures. Most of the audience would already have been familiar with the Stones' performances from the

group's increasingly frequent guest appearances on *Ready, Steady, Go!*, and the fact that the group clearly exceeded expectations could be attributed to their skill as musicians, and to the fact that they tried to play *for* an audience, rather than *at* them. An exciting style of presentation had evolved almost unconsciously. It was not something they had ever deliberately contrived or planned, but it is just what they had learnt during their Richmond residency.

Jagger, of course, was the centrepiece of the stage presentation, and as he added occasional bursts of harmonica to his surly vocals, so he induced fresh excitement and renewed bouts of screaming.

Phil Spector arrived in the UK towards the end of the tour, having telegraphed in advance, ordering the boys to leave his girls alone – instructions which were duly ignored by one and all.

Here was another case of mutual transatlantic admiration. At this time, the British clung to their inferiority complex in entertainment matters; Beatles apart, American acts were still held to be naturally superior. At the same time, of course, Americans felt that everything exciting in popular music seemed to be happening in Britain. It was a curious historical moment, when performers on each side of the Atlantic could imagine that the grass was greener over there, and it explained why Phil Spector was just as enthusiastic to meet the Rolling Stones as they were to meet him.

For a little while, Spector visited Britain regularly. His first visit to chaperone the Ronettes through the remainder of their UK dates with The Stones was, however, most auspiciously-timed from his point of view. It meant that when he returned to the States, he took the same plane that carried The Beatles to the US for their first visit there.

On January 17, The Stones released an EP – called, simply, *The Rolling Stones* – which they had cut in seven hours with Eric Easton producing. At that time, the conventional wisdom of the industry dictated that an artist release singles of straightforward commercial material, and LPs which allowed him the luxury of demonstrating the breadth of his repertoire. The Stones were not yet able to release an LP, and yet they wanted to avoid giving the impression that they had only singles material to offer. Thus, an EP was an acceptable compromise. It was not, however, a particularly acceptable EP, although it did well in the charts – even though retailing at twice the price of a single; but its overall standard was not high. One of the tracks was the Barrett song, *Money*, a powerful version of which had lately been released by The Beatles. Also, Decca stablemates Bern Elliott and the Fenmen had charted at the turn of the year with their rendition. The song itself, therefore, had hardly been keeping a low profile. Similarly, *Poison Ivy* was far from being recondite material that The Stones were bringing to the attention of the UK public. On the contrary, it had formed part of the staple diet of every self-respecting club band for at least a couple of years.

Jagger and Richard leave Chichester Magistrates
Court after answering drugs charges, 1967.

Not only were these tracks somewhat inessential; The Stones' versions were also lacklustre. The third track was a typically assertive cover of *Bye Bye Johnny*, with Keith Richard demonstrating again his confidence in tackling the Chuck Berry catalogue.

The whole EP, however, was made a mandatory purchase simply because of the presence of one track: Arthur Alexander's *You Better Move On*. Now, unlike Berry and the Coasters, Alexander was generally unknown in the UK, though The Beatles had covered *Anna* on their debut album, and Johnny Kidd had created a juke-box favourite with *A Shot Of Rhythm And Blues*. *You Better Move On*, an EP which might otherwise have caused The Stones' career to falter, notched up excellent sales at the time and is fondly remembered today.

After this, The Stones released their third single, the buoyant and infectious *Not Fade Away* in February 1964. This was an instant hit – both the recording itself and the increasing popularity of The Stones made certain of that.

All The Stones' early singles were difficult births, and this was no exception. This was despite the fact that Richard and Jagger had previously worked out a superb arrangement for the song – one that digressed so far from the Buddy Holly original that Oldham usually referred to it as the first Jagger-Richard composition proper. What they had done was to give the song their favourite Bo Diddley beat, with prominent use of maraccas (in the art of which, Jerome Green, Diddley's

own maraccas-man, had instructed Jagger). It was a conception that gave the tune a drive and an urgency it had not previously possessed.

Nevertheless the recording, at Regent Sound studios in Denmark Street, under the auspices of Andrew Oldham, was going badly. It was a listless session. Phil Spector was there, and two of the Hollies – Graham Nash and Allan Clarke – also turned up. Oldham telephoned Gene Pitney and asked him to drop by. Pitney was eager to do so, and his arrival – and the booze he brought with him – galvanised proceedings. Spector picked up the maraccas, and started shaking them violently, and the session went ahead almost without a hitch. Spector and Pitney between them had supplied the necessary inspiration. As it transpired, the recording was indeed an electric one, with an energy that was felt from the opening bars.

Spector also helped Jagger to create a B-side, a song called *Little By Little* that was clearly modelled on Jimmy Reed's *Shame, Shame, Shame*, and which the two had worked out in five minutes in the corridor outside. It must have given Jagger a lot of confidence in composition. Certainly, Phil's dismissive attitude to B-sides (he deliberately made them of throwaway quality, so that all radio stations would play the same side of the disc) briefly influenced Jagger – though he seemed more taken with the idea that 'new' songs could be created by tampering with existing ones; it made the creative process a little less arduous.

Jagger played harmonica, and Ian Stewart piano, on

Little By Little. Not Fade Away itself reached Number Three in the charts in March 1964. It was easily their biggest success to date.

There was a reverse side to this particular coin. Older generations were beginning to chafe at the group's influence over the young. After all, The Stones were deliberately flouting the social mores of the times: they wore their hair long; they dressed, even on stage, as the mood took them; and they made controversial statements to the press that were made all the more inflammatory by the unarguable logic they seemed to possess. In answer to questions about their stage clothes, for example, Jagger pointed out that, "From the time we started out at Richmond, everything we have done has been spontaneous. If we go on stage with a uniform, it is because we want to do it. We just act ourselves."

Why not? No-one had ever previously thought of granting self-determination to the young but The Stones had apparently done so; further, they were openly contemptuous of their supposed elders and betters, which made them, in some eyes, virtual revolutionaries. (Revolution was a more moderate concept in those days.)

If anything, it was the length of their hair which aroused most hostility. As awareness of The Stones, fed by a meddlesome press, osmosed throughout society, so the group became the butt of increasingly tedious and unimaginative jokes about their carefree attitude to tonsorial matters.

Even so, the nature of these jokes illustrated the difficulties that older generations were experiencing in assimilating the group. On the one hand, Jagger et al were derided for being excessively feminine. (Roy Carr's *Illustrated Record* features a photograph of Jagger under a hair-dryer in a women's hairdressing salon – no doubt one of the many that he wishes he'd never posed for.) There was also a tendency to denounce them for being virtually primeval – a cavemen-like quintet. Well, you couldn't have it both ways – not, of course, that that prevented the media from trying. Today, the expressions of moral outrage seem totally mystifying. At the time, the reactions seemed merely bigoted. The Stones, and Oldham in particular, were naturally skilled at turning such bigotry to their own advantage. Non-conformism became *de rigueur* for sixties youth, and The Stones were in the vanguard of that particular movement. Every parental jibe guaranteed the group an extra-loyal fan.

Jagger in turn kept up the pressure, and fanned the flames of moral indignation.

"We know a lot of people don't like us because they say we're scruffy and don't wash. So what? They don't have to come and look at us, do they? If they don't like us, they can keep away."

It was a long way from the polite and homely public image of The Beatles.

Nevertheless, it would be a mistake to imagine that in the early months such a crudely anti-authoritarian stance accrued wholly to their benefit. That would ignore the negative effects of their image. *Not Fade Away* for instance was so compelling it always sounded like a surefire No.1 record. Probably it would have reached the top had it not been for the fact that the strictures of some parents, declining permission for their children to buy Stones' records, were heeded. The antagonism of the middle-aged may have bolstered The Stones' cause; but in this sense it was simultaneously an inhibiting factor.

The group made another UK tour in February, with Jet Harris & Tony Meehan, Mike Sarne and John Leyton as supporting attractions. By then, The Stones were topping the bill on their own account.

For the next four months, the story was one of successive triumphs. In April they played two important UK dates – on the 18th, the *Ready, Steady, Go!*; Rave Mod Ball at the Empire Pool, Wembley, when police battled with fans outside the arena; and eight days later, at the same venue, they appeared at the *New Musical Express* poll-winners' concert, on a bill that was topped by The Beatles. On that occasion, whatever the pandemonium inside the auditorium, there were no problems outside it. In between these dates, The Stones had fitted in their first overseas engagement, at the International TV Festival in Montreux.

The other important event in their calendar for April 1964 was the release of their first album, *The Rolling Stones*, produced jointly by Oldham and Easton.

After the slight hiccough over the EP, The Stones made no mistake this time, and *The Rolling Stones* can take its place alongside *Please Please Me* as a debut album of outstanding quality. Between them, The Beatles and The Stones completely altered contemporary conceptions about albums. Until then, artists had taken singles seriously and treated albums as a luxury, using them for experimentation or (more frequently) self-indulgence. Few had approached the form feeling that the end product had to be consistently good. But The Beatles had changed all that by their determination to give both quality (they felt that *all* their recorded work must attain a high standard) and quantity (they made sure their LPs really were *long*-players; those of other artists began to seem medium-players by comparison). Apart from The Stones, the Searchers were the only other group to try to achieve such high standards from their album debut – but they lacked the finesse of their rivals. The Rolling Stones succeeded because of the interesting selection of blues and R&B material, and because The Stones were never prepared merely to put down slavish cover versions. They always added little instrumental frills that made their renditions special. Additionally, the production was excellent, with a full sound achieved on every track – Oldham could have congratulated himself (he probably did). Most of all, there were Jagger's vocals, which were extremely self-assured. He had learnt very quickly how to project his voice on record, and he had developed an undoubted lasciviousness of style, so that the innuendo and implicit sexual references – as, for example, in Slim Harpo's *I'm Your King Bee* – became all the more explicit. On a song like *Walkin' The Dog* he sounded really sassy, and thus put his own interpretation on a song even when facing competition from its originator (Rufus Thomas, in this case). In fact, *Walkin' The Dog*, which the group frequently performed on television, became one of the album's outstandingly popular tracks.

The other tracks included two of Chuck Berry's less well-known songs, *Carol* and *Route 66*, and Bo Diddley's *Mona*. The Stones, however, were slightly less discriminating in their choice of non-originals than The Beatles, who always went for the more *recherché* numbers. The latter, for example, would certainly never have covered Marvin Gaye's *Can I Get A Witness?*, which was already popular in the clubs. Nevertheless, The Stones' treatment gave it still wider promotion, and they also included an instrumental of their own derived from that source – a debt they acknowledged by titling it *Now I've Got A Witness* (*Like Uncle Phil and Uncle Gene*) – yet another reference to Spector and Pitney, who'd assisted on the sessions. Uncle? Yes, The Stones clearly saw themselves under tutelage. Meanwhile, *Can I Get A Witness?* became, with *Walkin' The Dog*, a regular stage number, and The Stones duly shared some of the credit with The Beatles for having brought Tamla Motown to a much wider audience in the UK.

In addition, there were versions of Muddy Waters' *I Just Want To Make Love To You* and Gene Allison's *You Can Make It If You Try*, which showed Jagger's increasing confidence in handling soul ballads which might previously have been thought the strict preserve of black singers. Jagger, more than anyone else, destroyed the myth that only those who were black and poor could sing the blues.

In some ways, the most encouraging track was *Tell Me (You're Coming Back)*. The song was strategically placed after the thoroughly rousing *Carol*, and the pair fitted together perfectly, since *Tell Me* was a slower, appealing ballad. What was encouraging about it was that it was the one real original composition on the album, and the first one of all actually credited to Jagger-Richard. If they thought it the first worthy enough to merit their own signature, they were right. It is an excellent track.

Oldham insisted upon an audacious packaging concept for the album. The front cover carried simply a photograph of the group, and was entirely bare of written information (other than the record label logo). Whatever the company's misgivings beforehand, the tactic was soon vindicated, as the album went straight to Number One, and stayed there for some months. In all respects, Oldham was emulating Brian Epstein. The important parallel was that each insisted upon promoting his own act as if it was unique, and that no show-business ground rules applied.

With The Stones' album at No.1, few noticed the quiet release of another track, *Surprise, Surprise*, on a Decca charity compilation. This was another Jagger-Richard composition, though a particularly uninspired one. Since the song was never considered suitable for orthodox release, criticism seems invidious, yet its tweeness does illustrate that Jagger and Richard were still very uncertain of their compositional abilities. The song itself, meanwhile, was soon treated with considerably more belligerence by Lulu and the Luvvers.

There were plans at this stage for The Stones to make a feature film. The Beatles, after all, had just completed shooting a *A Hard Day's Night*, and even though no-one could have predicted just how successful it would become, that particular path still seemed a natural one to take: artists who made sufficient impact in the popular music field were invited to try their luck in films, the cinema being the next field, logically, to conquer. After The Stones, of course, other groups did take just that course – The Dave Clark Five (with *Catch Us If You Can*) and Gerry & The Pacemakers (*Ferry 'Cross The Mersey*).

However, it never quite gelled for The Stones, despite the attractive proposals that were mooted for their film. It had been decided that they would write most of the music themselves, with Lionel Bart doing the screenplay. Later on, it was announced that Bart would also be producing, and there were well-founded rumours that Peter Sellers would be taking part. There followed a further press announcement that the film would consist partly of location work and partly of studio filming. Then, it was announced that all filming had been postponed until January 1965 – and, of course, it never did happen.

The first and most decisive cause of its delay was the success of the group in the States. An encouraging preliminary to this had been dates the group played in May thoughout the UK, when audience hysteria had reached fresh peaks. There was a teenage riot at Hamilton in Scotland, and in London at the East Ham Granada, largely because there were far more people trying to gain admittance than the venue could possibly accomodate. The tour also featured Duke D'Mond and the Barron Knights, a group which The Stones, and Richard in particular, had touted with great enthusiasm, and also Peter & Gordon, who had just then had a No.1 with their debut single, *World Without Love*. A chart-topper was something The Stones themselves had yet to achieve, yet the fervor of the fans during these dates was undeniable, and it was at this time that they were established as unquestionably the main challengers to The Beatles' supremacy.

By then, Jagger's stage style had been refined – whether shaking the maraccas vigorously, or just dancing, his was an inimitable presentation. It quickly became the routine which aspiring rock singers practised most keenly in front of their bedroom mirrors. In time, *Ready, Steady, Go!* would organise audience contests to discover who could best imitate

Top: *Thank Your Lucky Stars,* 1966; bottom: Mick
Jagger and Andrew Oldham prepare for a TV
appearance in 1965.

Jagger's stage gestures. The Stones were always a group, generally free of the fissile properties that dogged several others, but from this time on Jagger began to develop an ever more powerful image as the group's front-man.

It was the overwhelming success of this May UK tour which formed the background to the group's first US visit, where their reception was perhaps more mixed than they had bargained for.

Interest was greatest, naturally enough, in the major conurbations. The Stones were given the sort of warm send-off from London Airport which The Beatles had made obligatory for departing groups, and there was a similarly impassioned reception committee to greet their arrival at Kennedy Airport in New York. The Stones were mobbed for the duration of their stay in the city, as they found themselves fulfilling a demanding schedule of radio shows and press receptions. There was also an appearance on Dean Martin's TV show – a painfully embarrassing experience, since Martin made them the butt of jokes that were puerile even by the prevailing standards of American television.

Outside New York, however, little was known of the group – not surprisingly, since they had not yet chalked up any hit records – and they played to poor audiences on many of these ice-breaking dates. However, the tour, which had opened in San Bernadino with Bobby Vee, the Chiffons and Bobby Goldsboro also on the bill, concluded climactically back in New York at Carnegie Hall.

In Chicago, also, the group was rapturously welcomed, and caused headaches for the local police force. They also fulfilled a great ambition there, by recording at the Chess studios, with the much-respected Ron Malo at the production controls. Their cup was overflowing when Muddy Waters, Willie Dixon and Chuck Berry stopped by to assess their progress and lend moral support.

The sessions were a crucial step in the band's musical development. Up until then, there had been difficulties in recording, but they resolved all their problems in Chicago – largely, one suspects, because America was more attuned to the kinds of sound that The Stones were trying to produce. The sessions also galvanised Brian Jones, who after all had been the most purist Stone, the one most steeped in the traditions and romance of Chicago Southside blues. Working in his spiritual home, he made telling contributions to most numbers, often by adding a particularly charming extra layer of instrumentation – Oldham referred to it as a 'decorative effect'. His work helped to give depth and colour to the material, and certainly helped to broaden the appeal of the band. The rest of the group, too, were inspired by being able to work in such ideal conditions, and throughout the sessions the overall playing was at its most comfortable and assured.

As far as UK audiences were concerned, the sessions resulted in an EP's-worth of tracks, together with the next Stones single, *It's All Over Now*. This was released

on June 26, and it marked the beginning of a new era of great confidence. Clearly, the American connection had worked, and the single was a fresh and supple treatment of the song written by Bobby Womack and recorded by his group, the Valentinos.

The EP – which, true to form, featured nothing on its cover but a group photo and a label logo – arrived in August. It contained five first-rate tracks – one, *Around And Around*, direct from the Chuck Berry repertoire, and another, *Confessin' The Blues*, a Jay McShann song that Berry had recorded in the same studio some four years earlier. Also included was a version of Wilson Pickett's *If You Need Me*, together with two new songs credited to the Nanker/Phelge partnership One was *2120 South Michigan Avenue* (the address of the studios), an instrumental featuring Ian Stewart on organ (he also complemented Jagger's vocals effectively on *If You Need Me*) and the other, *Empty Heart*, which showed that Jagger and Richard were becoming sufficiently *au fait* with song composition to tackle a potentially daunting task – writing their own R&B number on R&B's home territory.

By the time of the EP's release, more pages had already been written in The Stones' turbulent history. On the day of the release of *It's All Over Now*, they topped a bill that featured John Mayall's Bluesbreakers, John Lee Hooker and, again, the Barron Knights, at an All-Night Rave at Alexandra Palace, London. The following day, they all appeared live on *Juke Box Jury*, as the complete panel of a new release programme which at that time attracted audiences of up to fourteen million.

Their appearance caused a furore. In making comment and passing judgement on recordings by their peers, The Stones had been a little too candid; they were also thought to have been slovenly, and not at all respectful. They were described as 'rude' and 'disgusting'. What there had actually been to complain about, never did become clear. The press and the public simply goaded each other to expressions of outrage. The incident nearly illustrated how Oldham had successfully made the five into *bêtes noires*. The BBC itself was not unduly worried. The producers had not expected a sophisticated programme, said an official spokesman, and they did not get one.

The next month The Stones managed to provoke a full-scale riot at the Empress Ballroom, Blackpool – more unfavourable nationwide publicity. This, however, coincided with the ascent of *It's All Over Now* to the No.1 position in the charts. It arrived at a particularly golden moment in pop's history; it followed the Animals' *House Of The Rising Sun* to the No.1 spot, and was deposed by The Beatles' *A Hard Day's Night*, which was itself replaced by Manfred Mann's *Do Wah Diddy Diddy*. In fact, *It's All Over Now* and *House Of The Rising Sun* between them established a trend for longer singles – they had proved that songs of over three minutes' duration could get airplay and could reach No.1.

The Rolling Stones fly into Heathrow after their 1966 European tour. Jagger's dark glasses hide a black eye he received from a flying chair-back in Paris.

Friday August 7 1964 was especially memorable. The group appeared on *Ready, Steady, Go!*, to help celebrate its first anniversary, and then, having made a split-second flight from the studio (though their car was divested of one of its doors as they were making their getaway), were driven to Richmond, where they were topping the bill on the opening night of the 4th annual National Jazz & Blues Festival. Both engagements were by way of particular thank-yous. The Richmond blues club, the Crawdaddy, had by then switched to the Athletic grounds, the Festival site, simply because of the popularity bequeathed to it by The Stones' residency;

Ready, Steady, Go! had, at a different level, been an equally valuable launching-pad for the group.

The festival was televised, and The Stones played a 45-minute set (par for the course in those days) before being taken by helicopter to London airport in readiness for a flight to Amsterdam the following day. It is a schedule which gives some insight into the hectic life the group was leading, little over a year after their first hit single. Britain and Europe had been conquered – The Stones' Continental tour that August was marked by hysterical scenes everywhere they appeared – and America was on the point of following. Eric Easton was carefully sifting the cables from the innumerable promoters desperate to take the group back there.

Meanwhile, Jagger and Richard had taken a further step towards being recognised as songwriters of distinction, when Marianne Faithfull took their song, *As Tears Go By*, into the Top Ten. Once again, it was the kind of song they tended to give away, since it was a lachrymose ballad, the kind of traditional pop fare with which they wouldn't have wanted The Stones to be closely identified. Nevertheless, the song marked a pronounced step forward, since it did have a particularly attractive tune, and it was no surprise that it should have been so successful. The Stones subsequently did release their own version, as the B-side of *19th Nervous Breakdown*, and later on *Big Hits (High Tide And Green Grass)*.

Mention of *As Tears Go By* marks the first appearance of Marianne Faithfull in Mick Jagger's story. Born in London, the daughter of an Austrian princess, she was seventeen-years-old at the time, and still at convent school. She had been discovered, literally at a fashionable party, by Andrew Oldham, who was attracted because the very chasteness of her personality. Blonde, innocent, and unspoiled, she was the complete opposite of the image he had used for The Stones.

Ironically, Marianne's own image deteriorated rapidly from 'purity' to 'depravity', such was the magnetic pull of the public personae of The Stones, with whom she could hardly avoid being associated.

Oldham, for his part, rejoiced in the knowledge that he had been able to launch a second act and, from this point on began making increasingly public noises about giving up co-management of The Stones (though he intended to continue producing them) to concentrate on discovering and moulding new talent.

Another Rolling Stones tour got under way in September. It was the most chaotic yet, as Stones hysteria reached a new pitch. The Beatles apart, the group was now in a league of its own. The authorities had great difficulty in controlling the crowds wherever they appeared, and there were particularly delirious scenes at Manchester, Liverpool, Carlisle and Edinburgh. Just as The Beatles had become accustomed to playing under a hail of jelly babies, so now gifts rained in on The Stones: sweets, peanuts, cuddly toys, etcetera. The actual set the group played, brief enough anyway, frequently had to be curtailed because audience excitement was so intense. Brian Jones relished the quasi-Beatles idolatry and remained the most provocative member of the group, frequently playing from the prow of the stage, coaxing the overwhelmingly female audience into emotional overdrive. Jagger tended to go through the act he had developed and appeared unperturbed by the mayhem in front of him.

After this tour, it was impossible for The Stones to continue playing ballrooms. The ballroom circuit had previously been the obvious one for popular music acts

to play – and thus it was at this time that the natural relationship between ballrooms and popular music became weakened. In other words, the ground was prepared for pop to become something other than dance music. After all, no-one could dance to the groups in ballrooms anyway, because of the press of the fanatical audience around the stage.

The September tour, on which Charlie & Inez Foxx, Billie Davis and the Mojos had also been featured, though barely noticed, duly found its way to Europe, where the scenes of pandemonium continued unabated – indeed, a riot in Paris when the Stones appeared at the Olympia Theatre suggested that they were perhaps intensified. The Belgian Minister of the Interior at first declined permission for The Stones to perform in his country, because of the rioting that had become associated with them. Needless to say, such action also fanned the flames of press interest and, with it, juvenile excitement. When the ban was lifted, the group was greeted by a large crowd at the airport, and a large posse of reporters – and when they did appear live on television, performing numbers like *If You Need Me* and *Time Is On My Side*, the audience rushed the stage, causing the performance to be halted.

On October 20, the group returned to the UK, where they headlined at an all-night show at the Empire Pool, Wembley. Two days later, they flew across the Atlantic for their second US tour.

This time the reaction to the group – not just in selected centres, but across the country – was very different. It had been a relatively protracted process, but they had managed to break through in the country. (Strange to relate, but other English groups, Herman's Hermits, for example, were to enjoy an almost spontaneous success over there.) Since none of their early singles had been ideal for an American market, an album track, *Time Is On My Side* had been chosen for release as a single. This had been recorded back in May at Regent Sound studios, prior to the band's first US trip, though it had not yet been released in the UK.

Originally recorded by Irma Thomas, it proved to be the perfect release for the US, and duly reached No. 3 in the singles chart. But by then it hardly needed a hit single to establish the group: their reputation was sufficient. The Beatles had opened up all markets for British groups, and The Stones were able to take advantage of that while appearing not to do so – for both Oldham's conscientious determination to give them an independent image, and their own ability to plough a musical furrow distinct from The Beatles, enabled them to establish a separate identity. Although the pre-eminence of The Beatles weighed oppressively heavily on the individual members of the Stones, the public only rarely presumed them to be working in the Beatles' shadow.

This second tour was relatively lengthy, and thus allowed the group to build up a publicity momentum. Right from the moment of their arrival, when Mick was felled by a bouquet of flowers at the airport, the group knew their visit was keenly anticipated.

The largely-female audience went frantic at the group's opening show, at the Broadway Academy of Music, and a number of police were required to subdue the mass hysteria. The next day, an appearance on the *Ed Sullivan Show* became almost as legendary as The Beatles' had been earlier in the year – though (as usual with The Stones) for less salutary reasons. The audience became completely uncontrollable during *Around And Around* and, after Sullivan had briefly restored a semblance of order, chaos reigned again as The Stones went into their next number, which happened to be

December 1962 – in the old days all that Brian Jones (standing), Mick Jagger and Keith Richard needed for a good time was a couple of Chuck Berry photographs.

Time Is On My Side. Ed Sullivan appeared genuinely frightened by the incidents, and resolved that the group would never again appear on his show. He even threatened to bar all rock 'n' roll acts, and all teenagers from the audience. He did turn his threats into general ones, therefore, but even so he did blame The Stones in particular for having deliberately incited the audience.

Sullivan was not the only establishment figure to express profound disapproval of the group. The Mayor of Milwaukee indicated that he considered that it would be a sign of immorality to attend a Stones' concert, and the Mayor of Cleveland refused to believe that the group could be contributing anything to the city's 'culture and entertainment'. In each place, ticket sales at the concerts were adversely affected, and indeed, as in Britain, parental disapproval clearly had some deterrent effect. Oldham, though, pressed ahead with his strategy, firmly believing that bad publicity is good publicity. And, of course, by then it was too late to stop anyway.

Other events on The Stones tour should be mentioned: the band did more recording, having been greatly satisfied with their efforts the previous June, and returned to the Chess studios in Chicago, where they did *Little Red Rooster*, and also went to the RCA studios in Hollywood, which was to become one of their favourite recording haunts. It was there they met Jack Nitzsche, who worked at the studio and had earlier done arrangements for Phil Spector. Nitzsche played piano on two tracks, *Down Home Girl* and *Pain In My Heart*, and developed a cordial working relationship with the group.

The Stones also appeared on *Shindig*, the TV show started by Jack Good as a successful American equivalent of similar programmes he had pioneered in London, and made their first film.

The TAMI (Teenage Music International) Show was recorded in Electronovision, a technique which enabled television images to be transferred on to film. The concert took place at the Santa Monica Civic Auditorium, and contained a veritable plethora of stars: the Supremes, the Beach Boys, Chuck Berry, James Brown, Lesley Gore, Jan & Dean, Smokey Robinson & the Miracles, Gerry & the Pacemakers and Billy J. Kramer & the Dakotas. It is quite significant to realise that such a bill could be topped by the Stones, whose first major hit single was then still climbing the Top Forty.

Jagger was clearly impressed – as who wouldn't have been? – by the stage antics of James Brown, and his own performances became more expressive and energetic as a direct result. The film of course is still exciting to see today, though it has become a classic largely because it captured so many top-name acts at a relatively early stage of their development. But it was a seminal one in so far as it showed that reasonable sound and visual quality could be obtained at a live concert by relatively lightweight equipment. Thereafter, hand-held 16mm cameras and compact recording gear became increasingly important in the filming of live concerts.

For a UK audience, the American title of *The TAMI Show* was translated as *Teenage Command Performance*, though that seemed almost as meaningless, so the name was changed again, and this time The Stones' connection was made absolutely clear. Today, the film is fondly known to one and all as *Gather No Moss*.

One reason The Stones had been recording so dutifully in the US was that they needed material for a second album, and *12 x 5* was released there just as their tour was finishing. With national coverage of the group's activities still in full flood, the album could hardly fail, and it eventually settled at No. 3.

By the time the group returned to the UK, Jones was ill – an early sign that the temptations of the rock 'n' roll lifestyle were proving too much for him. All in all, the group's recent activities had been so demanding that they must have welcomed the cancellation of their next tour. They had been booked to play dates in South Africa, but the visit was called off once the group had made it clear that they would refuse to perform before segregated audiences.

Little Red Rooster was the group's next single release on November 13. It was reported to be Brian Jones' finest hour, as he realised his ambition of putting blues at the top of the charts. The song had been written by Willie Dixon, though popularised by Sam Cooke, and The Stones displayed great daring both in recording it in Chicago and inviting invidious comparisons with the 'real' blues singers living on the doorstep, and by releasing it as a single, since it could hardly have been described as a natural single.

Nevertheless, the decision was an important one, since it meant that The Stones could never be accused of deserting the music that had been their first love for the sake of commercial convenience; and also that, with new groups appearing over the horizon almost daily, The Stones had firmly placed themselves apart from everything else on the contemporary pop scene. In any case, it was delightful to see such an atmospheric song at No. 1. The B-side was another original, *Off The Hook*, and showed that the Jagger-Richard team, although not yet quite ready to unleash their first self-composed A-side, was making creditable headway.

Though the final weeks of 1964 were – by their frenetic standards – slightly less hectic, they did appear on both *Ready, Steady Go!* and *Thank Your Lucky Stars*, and in December, after months in which all attention had been directed to the three Stones in the front-line – Jagger, Jones and Richard – one of those in the back-line, Charlie Watts, both asserted his own presence, and reminded the audience of the special credentials of this group, by publishing a book in homage to the jazz saxophonist Charlie 'Yardbird' Parker: *Ode To A High-Flying Bird*.

4

By the beginning of 1965, The Stones were feted everywhere they went. Jagger was then still only twenty-one. He always maintained that it was his stable family background that enabled him to cope so well with such a rapid transformation of his personal affairs and with such a potentially disorientating lifestyle. Jagger has always seemed psychologically well-adjusted, and such strength of character became all the more necessary during the year, as the worldwide reaction to the group became all the more hysterical.

In early January, *Heart Of Stone* became the group's new US single, and the second to have been composed by Jagger and Richard – the first was *Tell Me (You're Coming Back)*. This was in line with the emerging policy of releasing slow material in the US, and faster songs in the UK. During this period it seemed a successful manoeuvre and *Heart Of Stone* was a fine composition; since it actually seemed like a soul ballad standard, many would have been surprised to learn of its provenance. Its sales, though, were perhaps disappointing; it did reach the US Top 20, but didn't climb almost to the top, as *Time Is On My Side* had done.

The group, meanwhile, was touring continuously and had begun the year with a brief visit to Ireland, where audiences displayed a somewhat violent appreciation of their music: Jones and Wyman only just escaped injury from flying missiles (respectively, a shoe and an ash-tray – strange tokens of affection) and Jagger himself was struck on the thigh by an iron bolt.

Just as well, perhaps, that the itinerary provided for a week's respite after the Irish tour before resuming engagements elsewhere. Not that the seven-day interval could have been considered a holiday, for it coincided with the release of their second album, and they were naturally engaged in publicity work on its behalf.

The album might have been released before Christmas (after all, it contained much the same material as the US album, *12 x 5*, which had been), but in the end Oldham, adding finishing touches, had delayed it until the new year. This may just have been shrewd commercial calculation – it avoided the possibility of coming off second-best to the Beatles, whose own new album (*Beatles For Sale*) hit the shops just before Christmas. (It is worth noting that throughout these years of intense activity the Beatles and Stones camps always tried to avoid the simultaneous release of their records.)

So, *Rolling Stones No.2.*, as it was unimaginatively titled, did indeed top the album charts (in the event it was at Number One for ten weeks, just failing to emulate the eleven weeks that *Beatles For Sale* stayed

there). Like its predecessor, it offered simply a logo and a photograph on the front cover. However, the respective photographs illustrated the way in which the group's image was being moulded, because this time there was something unsettling about the shot. There were no smiles from The Stones, of course, and just a hint of menace. Richard's face occupied the forefront of the picture, which only highlighted his poor complexion. The group appeared neither friendly nor glamorous. It was the most deliberate break yet with the glossy world of show-business convention. At the same time – and The Stones' history reverberates with such contradictions – the photograph had been taken by David Bailey, one of the most fashionable names of the time and someone whose work would ultimately chronicle the chic glamour of the swinging Sixties society.

The menace hinted at on the front was made only too explicit in Oldham's sleeve-notes on the back. Oldham, who had by this time given himself a middle name, Loog, to boost his personal charisma, had written the piece in what he fondly assumed to be a kind of hip argot. Though the results were tiresome and pretentious, their deliberate obscurity nevertheless foxed Decca, who printed the piece without alteration or comment.

In fact, once the prose had been unravelled, it became clear that it contained a parenthetical passage advising prospective buyers to beat up and rob blind beggars, if necessary, to obtain the money to purchase the record. Needless to say, the passage goaded the establishment, as had been intended, and there was a furious reaction which, if nothing else, left Decca with egg all over its corporate face. There were, inevitably, questions in the House.

(Whenever authors of social history employ this phrase in reporting a particular subject, it is clear that they are thereby trying to convey the magnitude of public concern. As it happens, the fact that the matter to hand was raised in parliament proved nothing of the sort, for backbench M.P.s habitually eschew matters of historical weight to concentrate on trivial, passing ones – as in this case.)

The press created a furore. Decca immediately reissued the record, with sleeve-notes from which the offending passage had been deleted. It was all too predictable, of course, and it was all grist to Oldham's mill. (After some years, the record was reissued again with the sleeve-notes in their original form.)

But what of the music? It did not represent a great leap forward, but it was still exceptionally good. The sources were roughly the same – there were two numbers which Chuck Berry had recorded, *You Can't Catch Me* and *Down The Road Apiece* (the latter of which had been recorded in his presence) and a Muddy Waters song, *I Can't Be Satisfied*. There was a familiar Drifters' song, *Under The Boardwalk*, though not even The Stones were able to emulate the atmospheric original. Songs like Dale Hawkins' *Suzie Q* just seemed to be making up the numbers.

Nevertheless, a move away from R&B towards soul could be discerned – The Stones no doubt being mindful both that the soul style seemed to pay greater dividends in the US, and also that back in England the R&B scene was desperately overcrowded and overexposed, and a slight shift of emphasis was now called for. There was thus an Otis Redding song, *Pain In My Heart*, and the album opened with Solomon Burke's *Everybody Needs Somebody To Love*, another of those songs which only a white singer as self-assured as Jagger would have contemplated, since few would have been able to bring off the spoken intro convincingly. Jagger could do it, however (Eric Burdon was another who could have managed it), and he performed the song creditably not only on record, but also on stage. Indeed, it was a natural choice for live performance and in all respects was an excellent selection. Burke was not really well-known and The Stones thus helped to bring the song to wider attention than it would otherwise have ever received – Burke himself being one of those great soul artists destined to remain in undeserved obscurity.

There were two other excellent non-originals, *Down Home Girl* and *Time Is On My Side*, the latter of course having already been a US 45 release; but The Stones, like the Beatles, maintained a policy of not including previously-released British singles on an album. (The policy could not really have applied in the US, where so much more product was demanded; it was also only fair to make *Time* available to a UK audience at last.)

The album was completed by three Jagger-Richard originals, the first of which, *Off The Hook* came close to undermining the strategy outlined above, since it had been the B-side of *Little Red Rooster*. It was the strongest of the three, the other two, *Grown Up Wrong* and *What A Shame* being derivative and slight, although reasonably tuneful.

No, *No. 2* was not a masterpiece, but it was a perfectly adequate follow-up which served The Stones well. Oldham's sleeve-note manoeuvre had won the record far more publicity than it would have received in normal circumstances, and it benefitted accordingly.

It had been recorded, bit by bit, in what were then the Stones' three favourite studio locations – Regent Sound, London; Chess, Chicago; and RCA, Hollywood. Within two days of its release, The Stones were back in the studios, such was the unremitting pressure. They had stopped off in Los Angeles on their way to a tour of Australia and the Far East with Roy Orbison. Both Phil Spector and Jack Nitzsche, as usual, were present as

The Stones laid down the two tracks that would become their next single, *The Last Time* and *Play With Fire*, both of which were Jagger-Richard compositions. In fact, those four – Jagger, Richard, Spector and Nitzsche – were the only ones playing on the latter; the other three had all dropped off to sleep, and no-one thought it necessary to rouse them.

When The Stones arrived at Sydney airport, to undertake their first Australian tour, they were rewarded with an exceptionally delirious reception, as three thousand young girls, apparently determined to outdo Stones' fans in other countries for riotous over-excitement, mobbed the group and their entourage, destroying large numbers of airport safety barriers in the process.

This set the tone for what was, even by Stones' standards, an amazingly frenetic tour. While the group were besieged everywhere they went, the Australian press reacted with hostility to this dishevelled and discourteous group which was seemingly monopolising the affections of the country's maidenhood. The Stones rented a house overlooking Sydney harbour which had its own beach – a move that proved a mistake since it provided easy access for the hordes of Aussie hacks. The antipathy of the press (which, for once, Oldham had not deliberately fanned) did not, of course, diminish the great interest in the group, and the tour was a staggering success, with continuous requests from the promoter for them to fit in extra dates. The Stones played to over thirty thousand in just two days in Sydney, performing a set that included material like *Walkin' The Dog* and *Under The Boardwalk*, the latter proving tremendously popular there.

The scenes in Brisbane were less violent, though no less enthusiastic – Richard had his clothes ripped to shreds when the group appeared on stage. Teenagers were banned from welcoming the group to Melbourne – though over a thousand did so anyway, and that night's concert was characterised by all the familiar scenes. Despite the fact that a private security force had been hired, girls still flung themselves at the stage in fits of desperate adulation, virtually undressing Jones and Richard; Jagger managed to stay clear of trouble.

After dates in New Zealand, where audiences were comparatively restrained, they returned to give extra shows in Melbourne before flying off to the Far East. In Singapore they gave a wild show and had lunch with the High Commissioner, before returning, via Tokyo and Honolulu, to Los Angeles, where they called again at the RCA studios. Jagger was keen to re-do his vocals on *The Last Time*.

This was an indication of the increasing professionalism with which The Stones – by which, it was increasingly clear, one meant Jagger and Richard – were beginning to regard their recordings. Indeed, *The Last Time* does mark a significant watershed, for it was the first Stones UK single to boast a Jagger-Richard composition as its A-side. The song itself was first-rate, and became part of the mod soundtrack for mid-sixties youth. Because of their Southern origins, the early Stones always seemed conspicuously to be a part of the mod movement – yet it should be noted that they were always careful never to get categorised, just as they had never wanted to wear uniforms of any description. On the front cover of *No.2* it's noticeable that the four whose shirts are visible are all wearing a different type of shirt-collar. This may seem a small point, but it is not an insignificant one. The Stones believed that if they became too closely associated with a particular trend, then they would die with that trend. Thus, they went to some lengths to ensure that they avoided classification.

The Last Time was sung with great verve, and together with *Walkin' The Dog*, became the song from the group's early repertoire which brought to mind most readily the stage performances of the young Jagger.

The B-side, *Play With Fire*, was also interesting, since it was more lyrically adventurous – a development for which Jagger surely takes the credit. Roy Carr, in *The Illustrated Record*, refers to it as "an extremely underrated and atmospheric cameo of Kings Road society in the mid-sixties". Certainly, there were rumours that the song referred to Marianne Faithfull.

Dave Hassinger, who engineered much of The Stones material during this period, has referred to the growing confidence of Jagger and Richard, and to the fact that they were the two who made all the crucial decisions in the studio – the other three were only peripherally involved. Oldham, too, deferred to them. His role lay in trying to whip up the enthusiasm and excitement in the band that enabled them to produce their best work.

The Last Time was clearly the most commercial Stones single to date, and accordingly it reached Number One more quickly than any of the others. On the day of its release, the group appeared on *Ready, Steady, Go!*, playing both sides of the single and *Everybody Needs Somebody*, although the vocals on this were lost, since Jagger was buried under a surging maelstrom of feminine flesh. That weekend there was another television appearance – on the late-night *Eamonn Andrews Show*. The Stones chatted briefly with Eamonn, although it would be stretching the point to say that a dialogue was established.

Shortly afterwards, the group hit the road once more, for their fifth UK tour which opened on March 5th. Since they had the Number One single, it was perfect timing.

Supporting them were Dave Berry, Goldie & the Gingerbreads, and the Hollies – the tour exposure helped the latter to their first (and only) Number One.

The dates were simply crazy, providing abundant evidence of the hysteria that Stones' concerts tended to induce. The single most notable incident occurred in Manchester just two days into the tour when one girl flung herself off the balcony. This was not untypical of the fevered, highly-charged over-reactions. Jagger would barely be able to get through the first line of the opening song before the screams drowned out the music, and the girls rushed the stage. Sometimes, The Stones would have no option but to conclude their performance there and then. ("Three bars," said Wyman, "and we'd be back in the hotel with a thousand quid".) At other times, they'd carry on, in which case interest in the music became subsidiary to interest in the struggle being enacted beneath the stage between the besotted audience and the security police, with the St. John's Ambulance team on the side-lines, ferrying the casualties from the scene of the action. All this for a

Phil Spector (left), Gene Pitney (foreground) and The Stones enjoy a convivial drink.

performance which never lasted over thirty minutes, even if given in its entirety.

The Manchester date was also remembered for something considerably more mundane than the free-fall of one member of the audience: they were all barred from the restaurant of the hotel in which they were staying because they weren't wearing ties; no tie, no meal. It was just another of those incidents where the Stones fell foul of petty officialdom and, needless to say, it was faithfully reported in the papers and on news bulletins.

A brief Scandinavian tour had been squeezed into the schedules at the end of March, and it was almost a fateful one. While warming up for a show in Odense, Denmark, Bill Wyman was knocked unconscious by a 220-volt shock. Jagger had picked up two live microphones simultaneously and they had short-circuited, throwing him against Brian Jones, who in turn had fallen against Wyman. The only thing that had saved Jagger, apparently, was the fact that he had pulled one of the plugs from its socket as he fell. Wyman soon recovered consciousness, but the incident had been an alarming one. Neither was it the last that year.

Otherwise the tour could be accounted a great success, with audience reception throughout reaching its customary level of overload. There was one difference, Jagger believed: the proportion of males in the audience seemed higher than elsewhere.

On their return, they had another UK television date, on the revamped *Ready, Steady Goes Live*. The programme, which was always in the vanguard of TV rock shows, had decided to come clean and ban miming. Nothing could have suited The Stones better. Having been associated with the programme almost since its inception, they were a natural choice to help launch the new format – especially since they could obviously be guaranteed to derive maximum benefit from the programme's new requirements.

They spent Easter in Paris, performing throughout the holiday weekend at the Olympia, where audience reaction was utterly ecstatic. Françoise Hardy, the most fashionable French singer of the time, was in attendance throughout.

Back home, there were decisions to be made about the course of the group's career. This meant on the one hand that an opportunity to top the bill on UK's television's most popular variety show *Sunday Night At The London Palladium*, was declined – because The Stones considered it a family show (which it undoubtedly was) to which their act was not suited. This was an exemplary decision. The Beatles had once appeared on the show, but rejected all advances to return, and such refusals were more important than they seemed – they demonstrated just how the Beatles and The Stones had transformed the face of British popular entertainment by discovering and appealing to their own constituency. Previously, it would have been unthinkable for an act to have spurned such an invitation; everything could have been absorbed within the ambit of "family entertainment".

Later in April, The Stones embarked on their third North American tour, playing dates in Canada as well as the US. The schedule, once again, would have made many of today's superstars blench. The first date, in Montreal, was played on the evening of April 22; The Stones had only flown from the UK that morning.

Crowd reactions were typically ecstatic. Like the UK, French and Scandinavian ones, this particular tour was distinguished by a series of wild scenes involving uncontrollable fans, and by a number of alarming incidents.

During the Ottawa show, for example, the police kept cutting the power, a tactic which failed to dampen the ardour of the audience; no-one seemed to notice that it was no longer possible to hear the group. In fact, fans continued to rush the stage, and the police responded by drawing up a fifty-strong phalanx in front of it. This meant that it was no longer possible for the audience either to see or hear the group. In London, Ontario, the power was again switched off, and this time The Stones were obliged to curtail their performance – though as they left the stage, Jagger made it clear that he held the police responsible for the suspension of activities. Such frank criticism of the police drew the usual crop of critical press reports. It was all water off a duck's back, of course; at the Maple Leaf Gardens in Toronto The Stones played to over sixteen thousand – their largest single audience to date.

The opening New York dates were all extremely successful, and marked by acceptable (rather than unacceptable) levels of hysteria. During the five days they spent there, their hotel was under constant siege from ardent admirers, many of whom tried all kinds of imaginative subterfuge to gain admission to the inner sanctum. There were, naturally, a few who succeeded.

Despite the unpleasantness that their last appearance had created, they were again lined up as guests on the *Ed Sullivan Show* – though Sullivan made a special request to Oldham, asking the boys to smarten themselves up and, as a safeguard against the kind of fervour that had so disrupted rehearsals the previous time, the boys were locked in their dressing-rooms for the twelve hours prior to transmission.

(As a rule of thumb, The Stones were prepared to bear indignities in the US they would never have dreamed of suffering back home in the UK. Although both they and Oldham were only too conscious of the size and importance of the market, it is clear that they were concerned not to create too many waves. Not quite a case of 'When in Rome. . . .'; more an example of prudent caution in a country where one cannot gauge with certainty the reactions of the populace.)

This time around the Sullivan transmission passed off without undue fuss. The host later informed Jagger that there had nevertheless been a stack of complaints from parents, though these have been more than offset by the vast number of favourable letters received from teenagers. Jagger expressed some mystification that the group should continue to arouse such wrath among parents, but he was being disingenuous. No group had ever done more to exploit the generation gap, and he knew it.

Their final engagement during this particular New York visit was a live appearance on a mock popularity contest TV show, *Beatles V. Rolling Stones*. The media seemed obsessed with such spurious competitions at the time and were forever trying to find ways of expressing the pop hierarchy in some kind of league table.

Some dates in the South followed – in Tampa, Florida, the audience once again became so hysterical that the police pulled the plugs on the show, this time after five songs – before the group took what was becoming a habitual recording break. They spent four exhausting days in the studio in Chicago and Los Angeles, laying down what were probably the most important tracks in their career.

They resumed live dates at the Civic Hall, in Long Beach, California. This time the gig was noted not for what occurred during it – but for what happened after it: the getaway limousine didn't get away. It became trapped, and was immediately thronged by members of the departing audience. It was, as unnerving experiences go, quite something. Frenzied fans swarmed around and on top of the car, and the five sweating Stones only avoided suffocation by pressing on the roof from underneath. The vehicle was completely immersed in a sea of writhing, flailing bodies. Most of the girls were doubtless as terrified as the car's occupants, and several suffered severe and permanent injuries as the police waded in, swinging their batons, to allow the battered limo to make good its belated escape. "Definitely the most frightening experience of my life," averred Richard.

The US tour was completed with three farewell shows in New York, which had been arranged by promoter Sid Bernstein (who also had the good fortune to handle all the Beatles' US concerts) as a response to the spectacular success of the opening dates of the tour.

The next month, The Rolling Stones delivered their third and, as it transpired, last EP. *Got Live If You Want It* contained material recorded on their March UK tour, including one track which was a simple audience chant of "We Want the Stones. . . .". Its inclusion for atmospheric (if not socio-historical) purposes was absolutely valid; its attribution to Nanker-Phelge was certainly not.

Oldham's determination to obtain an authentically live recording meant that the reproduction was poor – but he was working on the theory that what was lacking in technical perfection would be more than compensated for by sheer excitement, a theory that was rediscovered by the New Wave in 1977.

The EP was not a great success. After the scene-setting chant, there was a burst of *Everybody Needs Somebody*, before Jagger's pleading *Pain In My Heart* and *Route 66*. Side Two featured two songs new to The Stones' repertoire: Hank Snow's *I'm Movin' On*, once a staple of the trad jazz and skiffle clubs, here treated with Hawaiian guitar from Jones and harmonica from Jagger; and their own *I'm Alright*, which allowed Jagger to excite the audience into paroxysms of screaming. The EP was a good idea, but it was not particularly well executed.

The rest of June was taken up with a tour of Scotland. The riotous behaviour of the fans at those gigs caused hundreds of seats to be smashed, and theatres were invariably left in a state of total disorder. This prompted Jagger to comment that theatre seats were clearly not as durable as they should have been, an interesting example of buck-passing.

These dates were followed by ones in Scandinavia, and then some UK dates at seaside resorts in July. On August 1, the group gave its own show at the London Palladium.

That was the last in their series of spring/summer dates. There was, however, unfinished business still from their previous tour in March. After their last date in Romford, while driving back into London, they had stopped at a Stratford garage to use the toilet facilities. The car, a chauffeur-driven Daimler, was apparently carrying a large and rowdy number, and so the garage attendant felt justified in denying them the use of the toilet. The Stones involved – Jagger, Jones and Wyman – therefore directed a few choice expletives at the jobsworth, and relieved their condition against the nearest wall.

Had anyone else been involved the incident would naturally have been unrecorded. But it was The Stones – and so charges were brought against the three of them, and at the end of July each was duly fined three pounds (with fifteen pounds costs between them) after being found guilty of insulting behaviour. The fact that such a ridiculous matter not merely came to public attention, but actually went as far as the courts, merely demonstrated the antagonism which The Stones had aroused in certain sections of society.

What probably goaded those people more than anything was the mere fact that The Stones had licked the system. They had shown that it was possible to achieve success on your own terms in your chosen profession, and that they didn't need to "knuckle down" and "grow up" or serve long apprenticeships. Further, at this stage they were just beginning to acquire the trappings of success, which no doubt affronted their enemies all the more: Charlie Watts purchased a 16th century Sussex mansion from Lord Shawcross, who had been Attorney-General in Attlee's post-war Labour government; soon, Brian Jones would also buy himself a comfortable rural retreat. According to one newspaper report, the five were now fighting over copies of *Country Life*.

5

There was no watershed in The Beatles' recording career. They just went up, up and away on a gradient that remained steady. There was always *Sergeant Pepper*, of course, though that was more a conclusion than a watershed; thereafter, The Beatles dissolved into their individual components.

The Stones' progress could not have been more dissimilar. *(I Can't Get No) Satisfaction*, the single released in the UK on August 20, 1965, was a giant leap forward, and it still bestrides the band's recording career like a Colossus. That was an absolute watershed; everything the group had recorded up till then now sounds, to a greater or lesser extent, dated; everything they have done since still sounds fresh.

Furthermore, the record fundamentally altered contemporary perceptions about the group. With its release, they were finally elevated, like The Beatles, to the status of demi-gods. Prior to that, they'd been the outstanding name among the clutch of acts chasing The Beatles: The Animals, The Kinks, Manfred Mann, etcetera. From now on, they were up there with (although not alongside) The Beatles, in a super-league of their own.

Satisfaction was a seminal single, justly regarded as a classic. It had been written on the road during the group's third US tour; Richard says the riff which is the foundation of the song came to him in a hotel room. The group soon built on that basic beginning, although strangely they have said that it sounded initially like a folk protest song. For the first time, Jagger really let himself go with the lyrics, and said precisely what he felt like saying. The song was thus an incisive commentary on the sexual and psychological stresses lying beneath the surface of American life. It was, both lyrically and musically a precise modern and urban equivalent of a rural blues song, with the singer giving vent to the frustrations of humanity's lot; "blues words with a soul sound in a rock song" is how David Dalton described it.

There's a corollary to this lyrical analysis – which is that The Stones by this time, were virtually an American group, the transatlantic mirror of The Beatles, whose concerns always remained primarily British. Not only did The Stones record more or less exclusively in America, but their music itself was American, touched by American themes and delivered in an American style. Hardly any of their post *Satisfaction* recordings bear the stamp of a native English band: *Lady Jane* is one, and that is self-evidently an uncharacteristic work. It was as though they had simply become taken over by America, for that was the environment which seemed to suit them most comfortably, Mick Jagger's love of cricket

notwithstanding.

Satisfaction featured a raw and rough sound, which was the triumphant justification of all the hours they had put in American recording studios. A track had originally been laid down in Chicago, but the band flew to Los Angeles – this was on May 11 – to cut more material, and to work further on *Satisfaction*. Eventually, the most stunning arrangement emerged once Charlie Watts found a different tempo for the drums, and Keith Richard put his guitar through a Gibson fuzz-box, then a newly-available instrumental aid. That produced a really ferocious sound. In fact, there is a basic, more folk-styled track underneath it all, though it is so well buried it is virtually impossible to hear.

The rest was up to Jagger, and he was perfect, showing just how much he'd learned about delivery from the great masters of American soul like James Brown, Wilson Pickett and Otis Redding. Given that his technique was so immaculate, and that the lyrics were so much more honest, it's a contradiction that his vocals should be so little distinguished in the mix that the lyrics are virtually indecipherable. Both Dave Hassinger, the engineer, and Jack Nitzsche, found this mystifying at the time; the reason, of course, was that The Stones did not want to jeopardise their chances of getting radio air-play. (There was another more aesthetic reason; The Stones always maintained that they were a five-man group, and that Jagger's voice was just one of the instruments employed by the group, and should therefore take no particular precedence over any other. On the whole, though, it was the censorship fear which probably weighed the more heavily.)

This in itself was another facet of the American influence. The song was natural radio fodder – and that was something that was virtually unknown in the UK, where rock 'n' roll radio didn't really exist (and certainly, the triple alliance between rock 'n' roll, radio and cars had never been – and would never be – forged). John Lennon always noticed that American records were perfectly tailored to radio's requirements – he cited The Supremes' *Stop! In The Name Of Love* as a prime example – whereas British ones hardly ever were, and determined to bolster the production of Beatles' records accordingly. With *Satisfaction*, The Stones had really discovered the secret, to the extent that they quickly outstripped the indigenous American product. Thus, while the indistinct vocal line helped to give the song an overall muddy sound, the main reason it was buried is simple – the words were too risque '. What was the point of composing a classic rock radio song if the radio authorities banned it from the air-waves?

Keith Richard always maintained that the song had been based on one of the Tamla Motown evergreens, Martha & The Vandellas' *Dancing In The Street*, though few would have made the connection. The chords which powered the song had originally been heard by Richard as a horn riff, so it was doubly appropriate that

Otis Redding should have chosen to cover it. First of all, he was able to put the song in the kind of context in which Richard had originally conceived it, by using the legendary Memphis horns, heard on so many Stax recordings; and, secondly, it was a fitting way of demonstrating the extent to which the pupils had become the masters. Jagger had been so completely influenced by black music artists and sounds. Now the most celebrated soul artist of the era was raiding Jagger's own cupboard, taking some of the soul back. Redding's version was successful and well-conceived; probably no-one else could have recorded a valid cover version. It all emphasised the exciting cross-cultural currents that were flowing through rock at that time.

As though to underline the fact that The Stones were now, to all intents and purposes, an American quintet, *Satisfaction* was issued as a single in the US some time before it became available in the UK. Richard had never considered the song as a single, and was sceptical about its chances right until it was shooting through the US Hot 100. (Later on, Paul McCartney would feel similarly diffident about the commercial prospects of *Mull Of Kintyre*.) By the time it was issued in the UK in August, it had been at Number One in the US for five weeks. This was an unprecedented situation. UK fans would mutter resentfully whenever Beatles' records (as happened once or twice) were given an official US release date forty-eight hours ahead of the UK one. In this case, there was a gap of some three months – a matter of some sadness for the band's loyal following back home, who began to understand that the group had been lost to them.

However, the delayed UK release had another effect, and this was to whip up intense expectation throughout Britain. A Stones' record at Number One in the US that nobody in the UK had ever heard? In the event, *Satisfaction* had chalked up over two hundred and fifty thousand advance orders by the time it was released, and thus took over the home Number One position with measured ease. It dropped out of the charts in November 1965, but no-one could say that it's ever been away. Like the poor, *Satisfaction* is with us always.

It was only after *Satisfaction* that The Stones really began to make money – speaking in relative terms, of course; prior to that, they'd been making less than they should have been. Their revenue had been disappearing in a thousand and one directions, and *none* of their contracts was especially favourable. It is certainly true that few of the British artists who dominated the US charts so triumphantly during this period were enriched as a result.

Thus, Oldham had been zealous not only in encouraging Jagger and Richard to write for themselves, but in trying to sell their material to other artists – for this was a more certain way of making money.

In fact, several Jagger-Richard compositions had been given away, but virtually none had been hits. Lennon and

McCartney had bestowed largesse on many favoured artists; most of The Stones' gifts turned out to be duds. In 1964 Adrienne Posta recorded *Shang A Doo Lang*, The Greenbeats covered *You Must Be The One* and Bobby Jameson used two of their songs on a single, *All I Want Is My Baby* and *Each And Every Day*. These were all unsuccessful. (In each case, not merely the song itself, but the career of the artist floundered, as if a Stones' song was actually an ill-omen; though Adrienne Posta, having failed to become a pop singer, later turned successfully to acting.)

Oldham was finding it difficult to fulfil two of his pet aspirations. First of all, Jagger-Richard weren't quite blossoming into bespoke songwriters in the Lennon-McCartney mould and, secondly, he himself was not developing into a top freelance producer, a British Phil Spector. (It was usually Oldham who produced these alternative recordings of Jagger-Richard compositions.) In retrospect, the reason for this failure is plain: even the titles make it obvious that Jagger and Richard were trying to tailor their material to a particular market; all these songs were artificial compositions – *Shang A Doo Lang*, for God's sake? Once they started to compose naturally, they experienced few problems.

Most of the compositions covered by other artists during 1965 had actually been written earlier; The We Five's *Congratulations*, for instance. The Toggery Five did *I'd Much Rather Be With The Boys* – one of the last songs the group gave away – and Vashti covered *Some Things Just Stick In Your Mind*. Lulu recorded *Surprise, Surprise*. The Stones' own versions of all these songs have been issued at one time or another. Meanwhile, one of the very last to receive a Jagger-Richard composition, unbelievably, was Liverpool comedian Jimmy Tarbuck, who used *Wasting Time* as a B side.

There is just one exception to the general rule of under-achievement. The Mighty Avengers recorded two Jagger-Richard songs in 1964/5 – *So Much In Love* and *Blue Turns To Grey*. Chartwise, neither really succeeded (though the former did reach Number Forty-six) but the songs were both well-promoted, and the group briefly became a minor cult name. The songs were hardly major compositions, but they were agreeably tuneful, and are remembered (if at all) with some affection. Cliff Richard covered *Blue Turns To Grey* in 1966 and took it into the Top Twenty.

The latter was one of the tracks included on an album titled *The Rolling Stones Songbook Album*, credited to The Andrew Oldham Orchestra and Chorus. Altogether, there were eight original Stones' compositions. The ostensible aim of the album, according to its creator, was to demonstrate "that The Stones' music is not just a noise, but their melodies and idiom can stand up in any form". The latent aim, clearly, was to try to present The Stones' repertoire in a more commercially attractive format, in the hope of encouraging potentially lucrative cover versions.

As the album was being released, however, the financial concerns were being eased – first of all by the outstanding success of *Satisfaction*, and secondly by the recruitment to the Stones camp of Allen Klein. Nothing could have been more fortuitous – or so it seemed at the time.

Oldham had actually met Klein while making the rounds of publishers, trying to get a favourable royalty rate on outside material to boost the group's earnings. This was the second way in which steps were taken to boost the group's overall income. He would infer that a particular song they were intending to cover *could* become a single – if the percentages were right. In Klein's case he was trying to do some retrospective bargaining, since Klein handled the Kags music catalogue, which included *It's All Over Now*. Being such a powerful personality, Klein managed to turn the meeting on its head. Soon, he was the one doing the hard talking. His objective was clear: to take over the group itself.

His task was relatively easy. After all, Oldham would not have been meeting him in the first place had the group's financial affairs been *hunky dory*, but of course their finances were not as secure as was generally believed. There were always a thousand different ways in which overseas royalties could disappear. Klein apparently possessed great shrewdness and understanding in business matters; he was a forceful and dynamic personality, and he was American and could therefore be expected to be wise in the ways of US record companies. Oldham was captivated by his force of character, and became totally convinced of his suitability for the job. The following day, Jagger and Richard met Klein themselves and endorsed Oldham's opinion.

Two days later – this was August 28, 1965 – the group issued a press release about their business affairs. Oldham became sole manager of The Rolling Stones, and Eric Easton ceased to be associated with them; Allen Klein became business manager for both Oldham himself and The Stones. It was said that he would regularly cross the Atlantic in their interests.

The group was delighted. Klein seemed a marvellous idea, and of course he immediately seemed to bring them vast benefits. Partly this was due to *Satisfaction*, though it was also to do with the fact that The Stones' original two-year recording contract with Decca had expired the previous February, and Klein, who was not so much tough in negotiation as overbearing and nasty, was able to produce a much better one.

In contractual matters The Stones' experience contrasted greatly with The Beatles', who had originally been signed to EMI for a five-year term at an embarrassingly low royalty rate. From the beginning, The Stones had been able to benefit from The Beatles' huge popularity, for Oldham had been able to use it as leverage in winning a more acceptable rate for his group, even though it was a completely untried one.

Now, with the band's proven sales form and worldwide acclaim, allied to the staggering success of *Satisfaction* – all points which Klein would have rammed home – the group achieved another leap in their royalties: all while The Beatles remained on their original miserly rate.

Extra benefits were conferred on The Stones. In return for re-signing with the company, in both Britain and America, Decca agreed to make five million dollars available to finance five feature films for the group.

Thus, The Stones' business affairs were apparently placed on a much better footing. After working virtually non-stop at levels of astonishing pressure for over two years, they were about to be given appropriate remuneration for their efforts. Klein had promised to make them rich, rich, rich, and that was just what they wanted. Aside from the matter of the contract, Klein also negotiated better terms in better venues for their US tour that autumn. Oldham reckoned that it would be the first tour to pay worthwhile dividends, and that the six weeks of concerts and television appearances would yield the band over one-and-a-half million dollars.

As in so many other matters, Jones, Wyman and Watts had played no more than walk-on roles in events leading to the recruitment of Klein. Jagger and Richard had been the two to meet him, the ones who had been impressed by him, and the ones who had given him the thumbs-up. It seems, though, that in this particular brief Richard had deferred to Jagger. It was Mick who had really decided in favour of Klein. As the world now knows, it was a monstrous miscalculation that would cost dear. The Stones would lose heavily; so would The Beatles; so, ultimately, would the British record industry. Jagger's judgement in business affairs was not as far-sighted as he thought it was.

The facts of this case, though, do point to a certain avariciousness in Jagger's character: his eagerness to recruit Klein, and his readiness to believe that the group was being ripped off and that its financial prospects could be massively improved are evidence of this. He had always displayed great concern with personal wealth and possessions. Money, of course, has been a matter of singular importance for many a rock star. It is nevertheless difficult to escape the conclusion that it has been a subject of *especial* significance for Jagger.

Of course, the amount of money almost permanently available to Jagger from this time onwards has enabled him freely to indulge in the other great passion of his life: sport. It was a trait inherited from his father, no doubt. He's been far more involved in athletic activities than he's ever allowed the press (and therefore the public) to realise, preferring to live up to the image of the debauched, decadent rock star. Yet he has disciplined himself to take regular exercise, and has always enjoyed a number of sports. In Australia, for example, he regularly went water-skiing with Oldham, and it seems likely that one reason why, on the early tours, he was so favourably inclined towards granting at least some of the requests for extra dates was so that

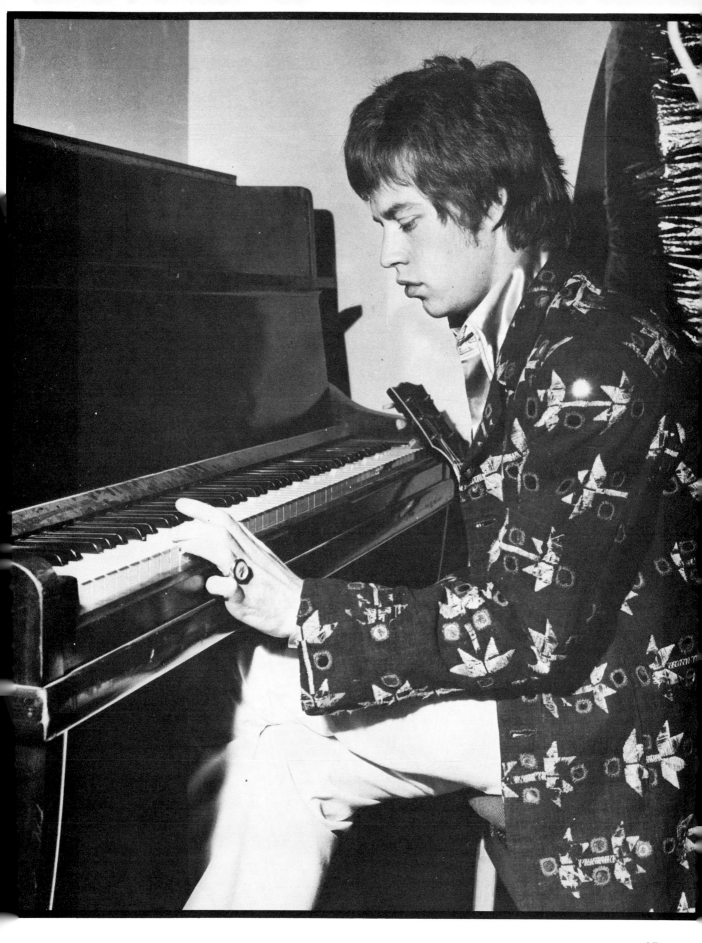

he could continue to avail himself of the country's sports facilities.

At the beginning of September, with *Satisfaction* racing towards the top of the UK charts, the group played two gigs in Ireland – in Belfast and Dublin. While there, they made a short film, *Charlie Is My Darling*, just a documentary record of those two dates. It had been shot by Peter Whitehead – who later made the well-received *Tonite Let's All Make Love In London* – and who also shot several promotional films for the group. The reasoning behind *Charlie Is My Darling* was that it would serve as the beginning of a video record of the band's career (an idea which, unhappily if not unexpectedly, was never properly continued, let alone brought to fulfillment). There was a second purpose, also, which is that it should serve as virtually a mock exercise for the launch of The Stones' film career proper – which, they all firmly believed, was just about to get under way.

The Stones' third UK album release, *Out Of Our Heads*, reached the shops on September 6, just as they were registering their fourth consecutive Number One single. It was The Stones' first major all-American LP, and by this time it had already been top of the US charts for six weeks (although it is difficult to suggest that it was in any way the same album; the track-listing differed substantially, and even a different cover photograph was used).

It was a very good album, fired by an electrifying opening number, *She Said Yeah*, and containing excellent soul material like Don Covay's *Mercy Mercy* and Sam Cooke's *Good Times*. The latter was taken at a seductively lilting pace, as Cooke himself did it, and yet The Stones' version was fresh and imaginative, recognisably their own, and one of the best-ever covers of a Cooke composition.

Their legion of fans would have expected a high standard for the overall work, and they would not have been disappointed. As a whole, the non-originals were chosen with some care, though there were the obligatory Chuck Berry and Tamla Motown covers: *Talkin' 'Bout You* and *Hitch Hike* respectively. There were four of their own compositions, self-effacingly tucked away at the end of each side. One was the already-appreciated *Heart Of Stone*, and another was the gently wry *The Under Assistant West Coast Promotion Man*, which had been the B side of *Satisfaction* in the US. (Oldham had reckoned that a UK audience would not appreciate something so obviously American, and so the replacement for the British market had been *The Spider And The Fly*.) The other two, *Gotta Get Away* and *I'm Free* were relatively nondescript, though with hindsight their misogynist sentiments are instructive.

It was a first-class album, featuring much interesting material, and all of it stamped by more classy vocal performances from Jagger. What would have most interested The Stones' camp, however, was its failure to top the album charts. It proved something less than

the irresistible force when it came up against the immovable object: The Beatles' *Help!*

That in itself would have indicated that some change was required, but that should have been apparent anyway. Their interpretations of soul numbers may have been skilful, but the very facility with which they pulled them off raised doubts about the group's true measure. Wasn't it a sign that the group was limiting itself too narrowly? The Beatles had long since abandoned cover versions in favour of albums that were all their own work, and The Stones would have to follow suit.

Not that there was any serious indication that Jagger and Richard were resting on their laurels; it was just a momentary impression. In fact, even as *Out Of Our Heads* was being released the group was jetting back across the Atlantic to lay down more recordings at the newly-opened RCA studios on Sunset Boulevard. This time, furthermore, the studio visit was the sole purpose of their transatlantic flight.

Since the group had a heavily overloaded schedule anyway, it might have seemed not only less expensive – in both money and time – but also actually simpler to have recorded down the road, as The Beatles did. But The Stones were enamoured of their American sound. Despite the seeming illogicality of the trip, the lengthy flight and the arduous workload that they were unnecessarily (as it seemed) incurring, they declined to record elsewhere. Oldham, of course, thought likewise, and there is no evidence that any of them ever baulked at the arrangements.

From L.A. they flew straight back to the Isle of Man to fulfil an engagement at the Palace Ballroom, Douglas. Their arrival was greeted with no more than the usual mayhem, yet this time they seemed to find it particularly exasperating – Jagger, especially, as he was only able to reach the stage at all by making an undignified entrance via a toilet window. He later took the opportunity to announce that it would be The Rolling Stones' last-ever ballroom gig.

Two days later an edition of *Ready, Steady, Goes Live* was screened which featured the five of them as programme hosts. Other guests included Manfred Mann, Goldie & The Gingerbreads, Chris Farlowe and Mickie Most, but The Stones themselves naturally dominated proceedings, performing tracks from the new album and allowing Jagger the chance to indulge in some light comedy with Andrew Oldham: the two of them donned an appropriate wardrobe and mimed to Sonny & Cher's *I Got You Babe*.

Ready Steady Goes Live may well have been genuinely live when it was recorded but by the time it was transmitted it was already a week old and The Stones had flown to the Continent.

One would scarcely have imagined that the level of hysteria surrounding Stones' concerts could have swelled still more. That, however, is just what did happen. There was a full-scale battle between police and fans when the group arrived at Düsseldorf airport.

Despite the fact that hoses were turned on the crowd, about two hundred devotees managed to reach the airport lounge where the group was holding a press conference that was necessarily abruptly terminated. At the concert, the fans were in similarly aggressive mood: not the kind of audience that actually needed incitement to riot. Jagger, though, went on stage and carried out a mock Hitler goose-stepping routine (apparently the frenzy of the German crowd earlier had moved Oldham to remark that it was all reminiscent of the Hitler Youth Movement) – which was rather like setting a lighted torch to highly inflammable chemicals. After the show, which Jagger and co. had fled in safety only by escaping through a secret underground passage (another adventitious reminder of World War II), particularly aggressive members of the audience went on the rampage throughout Düsseldorf, overturning one hundred and thirty cars and wrecking all trains leaving the city for the suburbs.

There was more. In Berlin the audience reduced to fire-wood the first fifty rows of seats, and it was reckoned that altogether twenty five thousand seats were demolished during a six-day tour. The rioting continued on the grand scale – it was the sort of behaviour that makes today's Leeds United football supporters seem positively genteel – and on several occasions the police turned high-pressure water hoses on to the fans, though without restoring order. At one point a diplomatic incident occurred when Stones' fans in West Berlin caused great damage to an East German train – with the result that the East German authorities attempted to claim damages from the West German government.

It was difficult to provide a rational explanation for such a high level of violence, though the disorders were generally attributed to the fact that The Stones had attracted a predominantly male audience in Germany. There was another development on that tour which received virtually no publicity at the time, but which is of some importance in the group's overall history. Anita Pallenberg was then introduced into The Stones' circle; she has not since strayed far from it.

She had been born in Italy and educated in Germany, and offered much to impress The Stones – and Brian Jones in particular. She moved freely in artistic circles, and had made contacts on the fringes of European cultural society, having actually first met Jones in the Paris flat of artist Donald Cammell (later known for his work with Jagger and Nicholas Roeg on *Performance*); she was suave, sophisticated and strikingly attractive. She was also resourceful and determined.

The Stones had a dual appeal: both a low-cultural one, to the mass of the record-buying public; and a high-cultural one, to those who considered themselves influential in matters of cultural chic. This may seem paradoxical, though in fact it was exactly the same for The Beatles. This explained part of the magnetism that attracted someone like Pallenberg to The Stones. From the time of her first, earlier meeting with Jones, she had

been determined to be taken on as a camp follower, and from this time on she was regularly at Jones' side, her force of personality enabling her to override the group's policy of discouraging female travelling companions.

Tickets for The Stones' sixth nationwide UK tour, which lasted from September 24 to October 16, were completely sold out within a matter of hours. Supporting attractions were headed by the very excellent Spencer Davis Group – though it must be admitted that the matter of who shared the bill with The Stones was of little significance.

The Stones' progress throughout Britain was as regal as it had been elsewhere. Opening night in London at the Finsbury Park Astoria was characterised by the customary scenes of audience hysteria, with most of the girls screaming and swooning. "Twenty girls were carried out unconscious after the rush in the first house," reported the *Rolling Stones Monthly*, "people queueing up for the second performance were amazed to see the foyer looking something like a first-aid centre with lines of girls being treated by the Red Cross."

The stage show, like the newly-released album, started exuberantly with *She Said Yeah*. After several other cuts from *Out Of Our Heads*, it concluded with two of the singles, *The Last Time* and *Satisfaction*, again and again. By that time, the audience was generally a surging mass of hysterical humanity. The stage would be littered with all kinds of gifts, some despatched with more affection than others. It's amazing to realise that despite all this, each performance nevertheless closed, rather incongruously, with the National Anthem.

Some of the dates were more remarkable than others: at Chester the fire-engines were called out to dampen the fans' ardour, and at Bristol Charlie Watts was virtually dragged from the stage, having declined to surrender his drum-kit piece by piece to souvenir-hunters. The behaviour at the Manchester shows was the most extravagant of all. One of the missiles aimed at the stage gave Jagger a nasty cut just below the left eye, and another (a soda bottle) actually knocked Richard unconscious. Both shows were perforce curtailed, and Jagger subsequently rebuked the police for dealing over-harshly with the fans.

In some places, the reaction was calmer, and overall there were some signs, despite the scenes mentioned above, that the tide of Stones-mania was not running as high as it had been. Jagger and the others seemed to take the stage in less truculent mood, and to acknowledge the audience in a more friendly way. Certainly, it was noticeable that the press reacted in a less overtly censorious manner, though whether reporters had revised their opinions of the group, or simply tired of Stones-baiting, is debatable.

The main reason The Stones had gone into the studios in early September had been to record a new single. Seven weeks later, the public had a chance to judge the results of the trip when *Get Off Of My Cloud* was released.

Clearly, this was a most important single, since The Stones did not wish to dissipate the momentum that *Satisfaction* had created for them. In the event, Jagger and Richard rose to the challenge triumphantly with a record that was almost equally forceful. It has an astonishing, driving power, with lyrics that continued the themes of disorientation and social alienation pursued on *Satisfaction*.

In every respect, it was a record to set alongside its predecessor, and it enjoyed an equivalent commercial triumph. To promote its release in the UK (where, of course, it followed hard on the heels of *Satisfaction*) The Stones made another appearance on *Ready, Steady Goes Live*. By the beginning of November, the disc was Number One on both sides of the Atlantic.

Their fourth North American tour got underway on October 29. Signs of Allen Klein's involvement were manifest. The concert dates tended to be more lucrative ones, in larger venues – an eminently sensible policy in view of the fact that the tour was sold out even before The Stones arrived in the country. More extravagant provision had been made for the group's own comfort during the tour; two floors had been booked at the Warwick Hotel in New York for the duration of their visit, and a private plane had been hired to transport them round the country.

Bill Wyman reported to the *New Musical Express* that the opening concert was one of the wildest in which he had participated. Fans broke through the security cordon and made a successful invasion of the stage. Though Jones, Jagger and Watts had managed to flee in time, both Wyman himself and Richard spent anxious minutes in the thick of the throng until police were able to rescue them. One of Watt's drums was stolen, and Richard almost lost his guitar; a vigilant Ian Stewart spotted the theft and fought his way through the crowd to retrieve it.

Despite this, the slight shift in emphasis that had been noted during the UK tour was evident in the US as well. Of course, audiences remained wild and reckless in demonstrating their support for the group, and teenage girls remained as pertinaceous and as inventive in their pursuit of the five Stones; but overall it was beginning to seem as though the German tour had represented the apogee of mindless Stones-mania. While the group was less haughty and provocative on stage, one could sense in the audience an inchoate wish actually to listen to the music.

It would be wrong to over-emphasise this change but, at the time, such signs were straws in the wind. As in Britain, the press seemed less eager to displease (though newspaper comment, naturally, still fell short of actual approbation), and Jagger was by now scoffing not at their sheer offensiveness but at their new-found desire to intellectualise the group. *Time* and *Newsweek* were both more sympathetic and suggested the group's examinations of the stresses of urban life gave them some affinity with the folk-protest movement.

Officialdom, too, seemed less unwelcoming. After a successful show in Denver, Colorado, the governor declared the following twenty-four hours to be Rolling Stones day. Similarly, the group was given the key to the city of Boston after a concert there.

On December 3, Richard was almost killed. While playing in Sacramento he received a substantial electric shock after attempting to manoeuvre a microphone with the neck of his guitar. Both the rest of the band and many of those in the audience thought he must have died – but he was saved by his footwear. Doctors advised him to rest, but he appeared on stage as usual the next day in San Jose.

The press was correct in attributing a growing intellectualism to the group, even if the band themselves, and Jagger in particular, remained publicly disdainful of anything that smacked of "culture". It was undeniable however, that The Stones were keeping classier company. In that respect, Pallenberg, who flew out from London to join the band in Los Angeles, was the first of many. In New York, Brian Jones socialised in his suite with Bob Dylan and Robbie Robertson (though whatever music they made together has been lost to history); and Jones and Richard both became acquainted with LSD at the Second Acid Test party organised by Ken Kesey and The Merry Pranksters after the group's San Jose concert.

At the end of the tour, the group entered the RCA studios once more. They spent four days recording new material – though on this occasion there was an essential difference. All the songs were Jagger-Richard originals, mostly written in hotel rooms in the early hours during the tour.

By the time they were due to return to the UK, there was such a demand for Stones' product in the US that As Tears Go By had been issued as a single. Jagger's vocals were supplemented solely by Keith on guitar and a string section. It had been recorded in London, with the arrangement by Mike Leander (who also arranged She's Leaving Home for Paul McCartney, and then worked with Gary Glitter during the seventies). It went Top Ten in the US, but Jagger always maintained that he never wanted it released in the UK because it would have given fresh ammunition to those who claimed that the group took all their tricks second-hand

from The Beatles. Such a comment would in that case have been apposite (even if unfair), since, earlier that year, McCartney had recorded Yesterday without the other Beatles, and with just a string section.

During the sixties The Stones were never quite able to provide a conclusive refutation of such allegations, but they must nevertheless have been comforted when Stevie Wonder – he was Little Stevie in those days – released one of his earliest major hits, Uptight, and gave much of the credit for its inspiration to The Stones and Satisfaction. He cited it, and Martha & The Vandellas' Nowhere To Run as the most important influences. The Stones had taken their lead from Tamla Motown; now, in the strangely circular world of the rock business, Motown was taking its cue from The Stones.

The group had worked incredibly hard during 1965, and they even worked their way into 1966, for as the New Year came round they were appearing live on Ready, Steady, Go's round-midnight TV special, The New Year Starts Here. The Kinks and a host of other guests were featured on this particular edition of the programme – a highly successful idea, though one which has not since been repeated.

It was hardly surprising, though, that The Stones should then have taken a month's holiday. The momentum built up again in February, following the release of a new single at the beginning of the month: 19th Nervous Breakdown. This was the third consecutive Jagger-Richard classic composition. The song is absolutely frenetic, driven along at a furious, un-danceable pace by some electrifying guitar from Richard and propelled, somewhere underneath it all, by

a sort of manic Jerry Lee Lewis country beat. The single is also recognised as one of the few tracks which allows one of the unsung heroes to step into a little limelight, for Wyman contributes some dexterous dive-bomber bass runs.

Jagger's voice was again deliberately mixed down to blend with the overall sound. Glyn Johns, who engineered the session, actually did a mix on which the vocals were more prominent, but the group rejected it. Even so, the lyrics were reasonably intelligible, and at least one drug reference could be clearly discerned. If the powers-that-be heard it, though, they ignored it. The record suffered no air-play ban. Perhaps by now The Stones could get away with almost anything, simply because it was automatically assumed that the words of all their songs were entirely incomprehensible.

The song's theme of psychological breakdown resumed the urban nightmare stance of the last two singles (and the title, unusually, had been conceived before the song itself; in the middle of the group's previous, exhausting US tour, Jagger had admitted to feeling frayed at the edges: "Dunno about you blokes, but I feel about ready for my nineteenth nervous breakdown"), but there had been some development. The emotions seemed less anarchic and slightly, just slightly, sympathetic. Nevertheless, the song overall represented a put-down of the kind of unstable, pill-popping, well-heeled girl who lives from one neurosis to the next. It was putting the boot in on a very specific type of middle-class girl, a type for which Jagger had particular animosity. There wasn't much humanity in The Stones' songs.

Jagger's growing obsession with such women illustrated that The Stones, for all the anti-establishment stance that had carried them through their early days, were now being assimilated by the very establishment forces they had railed against. They were in the process of becoming the house-band of the soi-disant; middle-class intelligentsia.

The B side of the single was As Tears Go By, belatedly receiving a UK release. (In the US, Sad Day served as the B side.)

The Stones made one appearance to promote the release of the single, appearing on the top-rated Eamonn Andrews Show. Jagger subsequently joined the other guests in conversation, and, to the apparent surprise of the watching millions, came across as affable, coherent and articulate. 'The following week, the Chairman of the Carl Alan Awards (one of which, Most Outstanding Group of 1965, had been taken by The Stones) made reference to his contribution: "I saw Mick Jagger on the Eamonn Andrews Show recently and he was neatly dressed, clean in appearance and spoke very intelligently." Nauseatingly patronising as such a comment was, it was nevertheless another straw in the wind; slowly but surely, representatives of conventional behaviour and conformist opinion were learning to love The Stones.

On February 18, the group's second tour of Australia and the Far East began. The journey there had not been direct. There were two stops en route – the first in New York, to appear on the Ed Sullivan Show again, and the second in Hawaii, for a concert.

In Australia, there were fewer problems on this occasion, largely because of stricter and more effective crowd control. All the shows were sold out, however, and interest in the group was as overwhelming as ever. In Brisbane, they made a film of themselves swimming and sunbathing on the beach, for inclusion on Top Of The Pops. Towards the end of February there was a resumption of more traditional patterns of audience behaviour when fans in New Zealand (who had, paradoxically, been the more reserved during the group's previous visit) rioted in Wellington. They took over the stage, and Richard was later treated for a cut eye.

As usual, The Stones interrupted the long flight back home to stop off at the RCA studios and record a batch of fresh material. As on the previous occasion, the group taped nothing but Jagger-Richard originals.

At the end of March, the group flew to France, for a European tour that was as traumatic as any of those of previous years. Their opening date, in Amsterdam at the Brabanthall Danbosche, was interrupted by rioting, and several fans were badly injured as police moved in. There were similar incidents during concerts in Brussels. Worse followed: concerts in France, at the Paris Olympia and in Marseilles, were really tempestuous affairs. Ten gendarmes were injured in Paris, and at one point a smoke bomb was thrown on stage. (It was rendered safe by ex-RAF officer Wyman.) Eighty-five fans were arrested, though all but one were released the following day; the lone detainee was charged with biting a policeman. In Marseilles the crowd rioted lustily, smashing seats and anything else to hand, and apparently even beating the police with their own truncheons. Jagger needed hospital treatment after being hit above the right eye by a flying chair, but declined to criticise the fans. "It was just enthusiasm," he explained to a Daily Sketch reporter.

The group subsequently played dates in Scandinavia. By this time, they had already been banned from three venues in Copenhagen, so they appeared at a fourth – but the fans rioted there as well.

The fruits of those sessions recorded early in March were unveiled to the public a little over a month later, when Aftermath appeared in the shops. (There was nothing especially significant or relevant about the title; it had been chosen in haste because Decca weren't able to stomach the original choice, Could You Walk On The Water?

It was the first Stones album to feature all their own material. Jagger and Richard, having fully overcome early feelings of inadequacy as composers, had now struck a rich creative vein. For there were fourteen tracks here, a total which even Lennon and McCartney had never exceeded, and moreover one of the fourteen lasted for over eleven minutes.

The standard of composition throughout was very high – a perfect illustration of how creativity and imaginative resources can actually flourish under conditions of intense pressure. The material had been recorded over two periods at the RCA studios, with the regular team of Oldham as producer, Dave Hassinger as engineer and Jack Nitzsche as arranger, keyboards-player and general all-round inspiration. The group used a greater range of instrumentation than previously (though Nitzsche and Ian Stewart, as usual, were the only non-group members heard on the record), which was immensely beneficial. Also Brian Jones demonstrated his aptitude for contributing an interesting coloration to a particular track by his choice of instrument – guitar, dulcimer, sitar, marimba etc. Thus while the fact that all the tracks were recorded consecutively in the same studio helped to give the album a uniformity, Jones' astute contributions provided an unexpected diversity and range; in other words, The Stones had achieved the best of both worlds.

Jagger and Richard had discovered the secret of knocking together a good tune, and *Aftermath* is distinguished by considerable melodic strengths – each track is individually memorable, though the two which made the most immediate impression (and which were the ones usually chosen by The Stones for promotion on television) were *Mother's Little Helper* and *Lady Jane*. Together, they represented the disparate qualities of the album. *Lady Jane* is a typical Stones composition, partly (as has already been mentioned) because of its pure Englishness, and partly becuse of its lyrics, in which Jagger assumes the role of supplicant. It was rare indeed for women to be placed on a pedestal in Jagger-Richard compositions. *Mother's Little Helper*, portraying neurotic and inadequate femininity, is much closer to the norm. The whole album is riddled with misogynist material. It's amazing, really, that The Stones had a female following at all. Girls were envisaged as being slatternly, insipid and subservient. They were taunted mercilessly: the girl who couldn't take care of herself (*Mother's Little Helper*), and the one who didn't know anything (*Stupid Girl*). *Under My Thumb* joyfully celebrates masculine domination in the sex war, while other songs like *Doncha Bother Me* seem to regard women as tiresome and insignificant – though perhaps the most wounding of all is *Out Of Time* – 'You're obsolete, my baby'; a cruel taunt, indeed, to those who rode on the fashion bandwagon – and those, indeed, tended to be the girls with whom The Stones were socially involved.

Mick and Keith were writing furiously. There was little time for revision or second thoughts; the lyrical preoccupations tended to reflect their true feelings. In any case, the tenor of the lyrics here is so strong that they undoubtedly represent Jagger's genuine feelings of hostility towards the opposite sex. "Mick's attitude towards women is that they are cattle," Richard told Barbara Charone. "They are goods – that's his basic attitude."

In one sense, Jagger had been betrayed by his artistry, since it was his concern to articulate genuine emotions rather than (as in the pre-Beatle conventional 'pop' songs) fake sentimentality that allowed his audience to see him for what he really was: a supreme male chauvinist. Previously there had been many hints, but it was the concentrated form of the message on *Aftermath* that left no room for doubt.

In accusing Jagger, rather than Richard, of anti-feminism, one is consciously attributing the authorship of the lyrics to him. This is as it should be. Jagger and Richard, like Lennon and McCartney, each provided both musical and lyrical input to a composition; but, unlike The Beatles' pair, their spheres of influence while working on a song did tend to be more closely defined. The music frequently tended to be a real collaborative effort, though Richard originated more songs, and he also tended to have the last word on the music, though it was nearly always Jagger who was responsible for the lyrics.

Since the *Aftermath* lyrics were so offensive, why was there no outcry? Why was the group's popularity not dented? There are two reasons. The first is that, in those days prior to the publication of Germaine Greer's *The Female Eunuch*, and other signposts of contemporary feminist literature, there was no real feminist consciousness; the contemporary women's lib movement was only just beginning to gather strength in America, and it had had no sizeable impact at all on UK womanhood. Thus, to a certain extent, women were continually being abused; it was a fact of life, and they were uncomplaining about it.

Nevertheless, the lyrics were so acute, and yet there was so little contemporary comment. The other explanation is that few people actually listened to the words of Rolling Stones records; the authorities who turned a deaf ear to lyrics that might have landed other groups in trouble knew what they were doing after all.

The point is a singularly interesting one for it shows that people responded to The Stones quite differently to The Beatles. The Beatles lyrics were listened to intently and, indeed, by *Rubber Soul* (at that time their latest album) were getting exceptionally good – and by the following year, on *Sergeant Pepper*, The Beatles would take the radical step of printing them on the album sleeve.

In contrast, The Stones' lyrics were barely noticed. This was partly the group's own fault. They had previously taken such pains to obscure them that many had simply given up trying to decipher them. Also, of course, it had been decided by common consent that it didn't really matter very much. Stones' records were for dancing, and no-one looked to them for metaphysical insights.

The positive side of the lyrics had already been hinted at: that Jagger was at least writing as truthfully as he knew how and, like Lennon and McCartney, he strove to avoid the well-entrenched cliche 's of pop

composition, and to introduce fresh lyrical values. Fundamental to this was a refusal to sentimentalise situations. David Dalton has remarked that The Stones were now writing with the "soul-searching irony and cynicism of the blues". Yes, but more than that, they were simply writing about what was real and what they knew themselves - that was the difference. However offensively it came out, it was the truth, as Jagger perceived it.

Of course, Jagger and Richard had initially tried to write hits under artificial circumstances – simply as product for other artists, but, apart from the Marianne Faithfull hit, they had experienced no success. Since they now quite definitely had their own songs to write, 1966 was the last year in which they were engaged as journeymen songwriters. Even then, the songs involved were generally ones written for their own purposes but on which they allowed others, as it were, to run the anchor leg.

One exception was *Sittin' On The Fence*, written for Twice As Much, a duo of whom Oldham thought highly. (They were, naturally, on his Immediate Label.) The song reached the Top 30 in July 1966, but didn't really have the success it deserved, for it was a worthwhile composition. The Stones' own version appeared in the US the following year, but not until September 1969 in the UK when it found space on the *Through The Past Darkly* compilation.

Jagger and Richard would not have lost sleep over its relative failure. At almost the same time they had a Number One hit with *Out Of Time*, which Chris Farlowe had recorded. Farlowe, another Immediate artist, received several of The Stones' songs before their own versions had been released. The first was *Think*, which he released as a 45 in January 1966. The song gave him a Top Fifty entry – hardly instant success – and it later appeared on *Aftermath*. It was another advance song from that album which gave him his real breakthrough, and then he undoubtedly benefited from the fact that Jagger had produced the record himself. In fact, the success of Farlowe's *Out Of Time* probably had more ramifications for The Stones' career than for Farlowe's own, because while the latter tended to remain a Big Voice with no suitable material, Jagger realised that he could handle production chores with great success; the death-knell of Oldham's involvement with the group was beginning to sound.

Jagger and Richard also allowed several of the as yet unreleased *Aftermath* tracks to appear on an Oldham special project: *Today's Pop Symphony*, which was credited to the Aranbee (ho, ho) Pop Symphony Orchestra under the direction of Keith Richard. Oldham's grand orchestral designs, which he pursued in the wake of his master, Phil Spector, never did come to fruition.

The song which The Stones had reserved from the *Aftermath* sessions for themselves, for future release as a single, was *Paint It Black*. Despite (or because of) the increasing acceptance of The Stones throughout society, Jagger and Richard continued to work on the theory that their work should nevertheless be found unacceptable, tasteless or offensive by *somebody*. Probably there were those who were affronted by the sheer morbidity of *Paint It Black*.

There are three interesting features of the music itself: one is that Jagger uses two 'voices' for the vocals, half-speaking to begin with, and then launching into his familiar frantic holler; another is Brian Jones' prominent use of the sitar, which only fortified John Lennons' claim that what The Beatles did today, The Rolling Stones would do tomorrow; and the third is that the influence of Jack Nitzsche, who'd been present at all The Stones' West Coast recording dates, was at its strongest on this track, since he offered the lead for the overall sound by playing the piano, as he said, "gypsy style".

Richard was never fully satisfied with the sound of the record, and commented, while the band were rehearsing for a promotional appearance on *Ready, Steady Goes Live*, that more time should be spent on it. On June 8, by which time *Paint It Black* was slipping down the UK charts, though it was still top in the US, Jagger collapsed from exhaustion shortly after moving into his new home near Regent's Park. He was officially said to be suffering from 'nervous stress', and was ordered to rest for two weeks.

Two weeks was exactly the length of time he had. After that, The Stones were due to embark on their fifth American tour.

The Beatles performed their last-ever live concert in Candlestick Park, San Francisco on August 29 1966. At roughly the same moment, The Stones imagined that they too were making final stage appearances. After fulfilling existing contracts, they intended to discontinue touring for the foreseeable future. Certainly, they intended this fifth US tour to be their last.

The fact that they and The Beatles had independently reached the same momentous decision illustrates just how physically and mentally taxing the whole touring process had become. By 1966, tours were a concentrated form of ritualised madness. The real world was temporarily held in suspension. The Stones-mania manifested by audiences the world over became mirrored in the backstage and off-duty behaviour of the group itself. In that rarefied and unreal atmosphere, almost any course of action became legitimate. Inevitably, The Stones and their camp were kept well supplied with the newly-fashionable drugs like marijuana and LSD – almost a necessary facility if they were to fulfil such an arduous schedule.

Even apart from understandable reasons for the prevailing atmosphere of quasi-insanity, The Stones themselves made self-conscious contributions to the generally deranged proceedings. It still behoved them to act outrageously, simply because they knew they would grasp generous publicity benefits from such behaviour. Although they no loner courted unfavourable press attention as assiduously as they had in the early days, they recognised that their cause was still assisted by the odd skirmish. Also, of course, they had never learned respect for the press, and could be rather cruel in their baiting of reporters.

The US tour itself had actually been preceded by a publicity stunt, courtesy of the combined imaginations of Klein and Oldham. By this time, The Stones were *personae non gratae* at most of the prestigious New York hotels. Not because of their own behaviour – after all, damage would always be paid for (and there were probably a number of hotels which used to rely on regular visits from the rock fraternity – Keith Moon, for example – to defray the costs of periodic redecoration); it was because of the horde of fans who'd inevitably discover the group's H.Q. and mount a permanent and, inevitably, noisy vigil outside it. This, needless to say, deterred others from using the hotel.

When therefore none of the first-choice hotels

seemed willing to accept reservations for the group, Oldham announced that he would be lodging a court action over the unofficial ban, and suing fourteen New York hotels for damages of five million dollars. The announcement obviously generated considerable publicity at the most favourable time of all – just prior to the group's arrival in the country. No such claim, of course, was ever filed. The accomodation difficulty was solved by Allen Klein, who made his own luxury yacht, *S. S. Sea Panther*, available during their visit.

The actual tour began in Lynn, Massachussetts (the town twenty miles north of Boston where, fans of rock 'n' roll trivia might like to know, Freddy Cannon was born) amid customary scenes of audience mayhem. Fans broke through a police cordon and stormed the outdoor stage. The police retaliated by firing tear gas grenades to try to keep them at bay. They hadn't reckoned on the direction of the wind, however, and the gas drifted towards the stage rather than the audience. After the concert, The Stones leapt straight into waiting cadillacs, but even then some fans tried to mount an attack on the vehicles, using planks taken from police barricades.

In Montreal, the security force incited the wrath of audience and group alike. Jagger at one point stopped the show to make a public complaint about their ill-treatment of members of the audience. The bouncers themselves were not amused, and The Stones' hasty exit afterwards was to avoid them as much as the audience.

The Stones inaugurated the 1966 Music Festival in New York. The very high temperatures did not induce drowsiness in the audience, and the occasion was marked by continuous rioting, with police freely using both truncheons and tear gas to combat the fans. Three days later, in Syracuse, New York, the group behaved with apparent discourtesy towards an American flag, by dragging it across the floor, and for once their espousal of unfavourable publicity threatened to inflict serious harm on the group's career, but the incident was successfully defused.

Meanwhile, the tour continued in the manner in which it had begun, with riots in several cities, including Vancouver, where a special police documentary had been shot on the occasion of the group's previous visit in the hope that the force would learn successful crowd control tactics from it. In the event, the audience riot in that city was one of the worst on the whole tour; though the general level of audience excitement also impels mention of the concerts at Chicago, Boston, St. Louis and Houston.

The three final concerts of the tour took place in Los Angeles, San Francisco and Hawaii, and passed off without incident. Except, that is, for Jagger's announcement from the stage in Honolulu that the concert which the band were then giving would be their last. Ever. At another time and in another place, the 'shock' announcement would have engendered considerable publicity. In fact, it was little reported –

no-one seemed to take Jagger seriously. And yet, as it transpired, it *was* the last concert in America given by the original Rolling Stones.

It had been altogether a strange tour for Brian Jones. On the one hand, relations with the rest of the group had been less strained – indeed, the entire tour was noted for a kind of rapprochement. Under the combined influence of hash and assorted chemicals, Jones, Jagger and Richard rekindled an understanding they had not known since the Edith Grove days. In some ways, Brian was behaving in a more mature fashion, and was actively looking for areas in which he could be creative. His purposeful and attractive contributions to *Aftermath* had clearly boosted his confidence. His relationship with Anita Pallenberg was doing wonders for his self-confidence. She clearly found favour with the others, and, indeed, Richard showed particular interest in her. Far from being jealous, Jones was merely happy that her arrival in the camp had coincided with the restoration of friendly relations.

The tour nevertheless had its negative aspects for Jones. His keen interest in drugs was already undermining his health, and he missed the entire mid-Western part of the itinerary – two weeks in all – because of illness. During that period, The Stones went out as a four-piece, with Richard ably compensating for

The Stones in Heathrow's departure lounge, 1967. Jagger and Richard were subsequently refused entry to the U.S. by immigration officials.

Jones' absence.

The American tour had been a kind of celebration, since all concerned knew that it would be their last bout of sustained activity for some time. On its conclusion, the five immediately went their separate ways, to take a month's well-earned holiday. Jones and Anita went to North Africa, to spend time in Tangier. It was while climbing in Morocco that he broke his left hand. This could have been a serious mishap, but in the event there was no need for Richard to do any more filling-in for Jones, and no group plans were affected. Jones' bandaged hand can be clearly seen on the front cover photograph of *High Tide and Green Grass*.

In September, the group reassembled after their separate vacations – Mick had been to Mexico, Keith to New York, Charlie to the Greek islands and Bill Wyman to Florida – for another appearance on the *Ed Sullivan Show*, and to prepare for the release of their next single, which had been recorded on August 3, at the conclusion of the US tour, and was due for release on September 23. For once, release in the US and UK was simultaneous.

Singles were traditionally supposed to have short, snappy titles. Long titles were considered 'difficult'. *Have You Seen Your Mother, Baby, Standing In The Shadow* was certainly a long title. It was the most immediate sign that this was indeed a 'difficult' single. Neither the public nor the record business quite knew what to make of it, and this uncertainty is reflected in the fact that it failed to top either the US or the UK charts.

This time, the words actually were indecipherable, though even if the vocals could have been made out it is unlikely that anyone would have been able to make sense of them. Andrew Oldham, for instance, virtually admitted that he hadn't understood them.

On first hearing, the song seemed to lack a distinct melody, but subsequent listenings brought out the latent power of the music. It was significant that the recording was made straight after the resounding success of Ike & Tina Turner's *River Deep, Mountain High*, generally considered to be Phil Spector's finest three minutes. *Have You Seen* was an attempt to pull off a Stones' equivalent of that fine work – to do something that was almost apocalyptic in its sensational use of sound. This was a cataclysmic tidal wave; a barrage of sound that cascaded down and engulfed the listener. The energy-level was simply astonishing.

It was utterly brilliant, and yet it didn't quite work. Keith Richard probably has the explanation, for he has always maintained that the version originally recorded was sublime, but that in the haste to get it into the shops, it was badly mixed. This sounds feasible, and, indeed, it is surprising that such mistakes did not exercise greater constraints on The Stones' recording career, because much of the material The Stones recorded was processed remarkably quickly. It is just a pity that it had to happen with this single. As it stands, it still seems something of an oddity in The Stones canon;

yet potentially it was the greatest single of them all.

After the somewhat unhappy reception accorded the single, The Stones back-tracked, and abandoned ideas about achieving a total, climactic sound – in just the same way as Spector himself, after the bewildering failure of *River Deep, Mountain High* in the US, abandoned his own work in the field. He went into retirement and seclusion; The Stones certainly didn't do that, but they never again looked to him as an influence.

The *Have You Seen Your Mother* episode, however, was not concerned solely with the music. Even more bizarre was the publicity material accompanying the record. In order to emphasise the 'Mother' aspect, the five of them dressed up in drag, assembled on New York's Park Avenue and had their photograph taken by Jerry Schatzberg. (He later became a successful film director, with *Panic In Needle Park*, *Puzzle Of A Downfall Child* and *Scarecrow* to his credit.) The shots were used to launch the single, and so it's quite conceivable that it was the type of publicity campaign, as much of the single itself, that explains its relative failure. There's some evidence that the average fan in the street misconstrued the intentions of the group; after all, transvestism itself had always been a 'difficult' concept for the public to accept.

The real joke about the photo-session was that after it was over, the five simply walked into an adjacent bar and ordered a round of beers. Nobody paid any attention to the oddly-dressed quintet. Schatzberg duly held a party for the group, which took place after their Ed Sullivan appearance. Did they turn up in drag again? No, in Nazi uniforms. Faced with the fact that their anti-social posturings of earlier days now seemed less unacceptable, and that the group itself almost respectable, their ill-judged attempts to stay one step ahead in outrage were becoming increasingly gauche.

On the day of the release of *Have You Seen Your Mother* the group embarked on the British dates that were intended to complete their touring engagements for the foreseeable future. Beyond this last tour lay an indefinite period of rest, to allow them to recover physically and emotionally from the fatigues of life on the road. Accompanying them were The Yardbirds and Ike & Tina Turner, both of them fitting support acts. The Yardbirds had a similar background in British blues, and had taken over The Stones' Richmond residency; at that time the line-up included Jeff Beck, Jimmy Page and Keith Relf. Ike & Tina were respected as much for their soul and blues recordings during the sixties as for their more recent work with Phil Spector. Both fields of interest overlapped with The Stones. They themselves were at full strength. Despite his hand injury, Brian Jones had passed a late fitness test.

The tour opened in triumph at the Royal Albert Hall in London. Being a conventional concert venue, access to the stage from the audience was relatively unhindered. No sooner had The Stones appeared than they found themselves surrounded. Keith Richard was buried beneath an avalanche of young girls – Ian Stewart loyally rescued him. Jagger, Jones and Wyman ran for it. It momentarily seemed as though the concert would be concluded before a note had been played.

In the event, a semblance of order was restored. The security staff cleared the stage. However, the fracas was immediately renewed when the group reappeared. Although The Stones' performance duly went ahead anyway, it was punctuated by kamikaze raids from members of the audience, flinging themselves onto the stage. The show went more or less to schedule, though certain ancillary plans were foiled by the fervour of the audience. It had been arranged that the group would be presented with no less than twenty-two gold discs, marking American sales of their records. It was thought prudent to leave this ceremony until afterwards, at the Kensington Hotel. Similarly, the group had hoped to record the performance for an American live album (to be given the same title, *Got Live If You Want It*, as the British EP released eighteen months earlier), but due to what Wyman described as the 'bloody riot' these plans were naturally aborted. In the event, only two tracks from the Albert Hall were thought suitable for the album.

Many other shows were equally as wild as the London one, with Manchester again the place where the stormiest scenes were recorded. It was at Bristol and Newcastle that Oldham and co. managed to tape material suitable enough for the US live album – though it must be said that The Stones, who have released some successful live albums in their career, were not unduly concerned about this one. It's an entirely disposable work.

The album simultaneously released in Britain was *Big Hits (High Tide and Green Grass)*, a compilation that had appeared some months earlier in the US, in a different form. Almost inevitably, the British version was preferable, since it contained a more comprehensive selection of tracks which included all the singles with the exception of *I Wanna Be Your Man*; allegations about the group's indebtedness to The Beatles had clearly drawn blood. Jagger was trying to pull a veil over the fact that The Beatles actually had provided a significant impetus to their early career. He encouraged the public to forget that The Stones had ever recorded the song, which was similarly omitted from every other compilation which The Stones themselves controlled.

In addition to the singles, there were four other tracks to ensure that the album offered real value-for-money: *Time Is On My Side*, *Heart Of Stone* and *As Tears Go By*, all Top Ten singles in the US, and *Lady Jane* from *Aftermath*.

The rock business has generated, among other things, an incredible number of 'Greatest Hits' albums. More compilation albums than there have been original hit singles in the first place. Not surprisingly, most contravene the Trade Descriptions Act, and only a few are satisfactory. *High Tide And Green Grass* stands out as one of the finest compilations ever made of the work of a top rock act. Strangely enough, it was infinitely superior to a parallel collection of The Beatles' hits, released almost simultaneously. Justice prevailed, and *High Tide* fared much better than *A Collection Of Beatles Oldies (But Goldies)*.

Perhaps one reason why The Stones' set was more satisfying is that The Beatles' one was not released at an especially fitting moment. It simply served to fill a particularly alarming gap in the company's Christmas release, for it provided the epilogue to the first stage of The Stones' career, which was now concluded. As the group prepared to take a well-earned rest, so the *Rolling Stones Monthly*, which had faithfully chronicled the exploits of its heroes since its inception in June 1964 ceased publication – an equally resounding confirmation of the fact that the group's career had reached its first hiatus.

The Stones prepare to escape from the London Palladium. Jagger was unrepentant about missing the show's revolving stage finale: 'That revolving stage isn't an altar – it's just a drag.'

60

Mick Jagger and Marianne Faithful arrive (late) for a
gala performance at the Royal Opera House,
London, 1967.

6

There was one other respect in which the end of 1966 marked a watershed in the life and career of Mick Jagger: he broke off his longstanding affair with Chrissie Shrimpton. He'd been going out with her for over three years – virtually right through the group's years of success, in fact. She was the younger sister of Jean Shrimpton who, prior to the emergence of Twiggy, was the country's most well-known model, and therefore the one most associated with the sixties styles that were beginning to make London the mecca of world fashion.

The country's pre-eminence in popular music was a parallel, inter-connected development. There was nevertheless a sense in which pop stars remained on the outside looking in. The Beatles had been the only ones to have crossed the socio-cultural divide that was a feature of the British class system. Jagger felt that The Stones deserved to be as culturally acceptable as The Beatles – and, as we have seen, the group was in the process of becoming so. It would have assisted Jagger's purpose for him to be going out with the sister of the country's fashion queen; it placed him only one remove away from the centre of high society.

As The Stones did become increasingly culturally acceptable, so Jagger began to experience a sense of frustration that he was not the consort of girls of greater social status. He thought that film stars should be accompanying him. Such feelings inevitably signalled the beginning of the end of his relationship with Chrissie.

Aside from her advantageous family connection, there is one other obvious explanation of why Mick went out with Chrissie for as long as he did: Chrissie willingly adopted the submissive role that Jagger expected of his women, and she was always available as a regular companion. Although Jagger yearned to be associating with women of some importance, the relationship with Chrissie was at least a secure one; Jagger's inertia and his lack of self-confidence ensured that the relationship lasted for over three years. The parting was strictly amicable and both emerged with their dignity intact. Mick: "Three years is a long time to be with someone, but although we were unofficially engaged we hadn't set any date for a wedding." Chrissie: "We were very much in love, but we argued all the time. As time goes on you begin to feel different about life and each other. There wasn't a row. We broke by mutual agreement."

What had hastened the split was Jagger's growing relationship with Marianne Faithfull – and in that, it seems, it was Marianne who wooed Mick rather than vice-versa. Jagger allowed himself to be seduced away,

and anyway an affair with Ms. Faithfull was good for sensational headlines, if for nothing else.

By December 1966, a strong social circle had emerged from the centre of the group; Wyman and Watts, almost inevitably, had no part in it. The circle was based on a large flat in Courtfield Road, which Jones had purchased to share with Anita. Jagger would be there with Marianne, and Richard would be on his own, having lately concluded business with Linda Keith, a longstanding American girlfriend. Celebrities who were invited into the clique included Robert Fraser, antique dealer Christopher Gibbs, photographer Michael Cooper and the men's wear entrepreneur Michael Rainey; also involved was Tara Guinness, the heir to the brewery fortune (who sadly died in a car accident the following year – an event The Beatles incorporated into *A Day In The Life*). Most of the entourage assembled in Paris that Christmas, where they had enormous fun at the Georges Cinq Hotel. The strains of touring were over, and they could begin to enjoy themselves. While Jones and Jagger had purchased flats in London, Richard had bought a large house in Sussex – Redlands in West Wittering – though it was only towards the end of the year that he had the time to move in.

The group had virtually completed all their engagements. The next album, *Between The Buttons*, was just about finished. There was just one outstanding matter: the group's feature film debut. Announcements concerning this had been despatched at regular intervals from the group's press office. But while the group's PR corps all kept their noses to the grindstone, the group itself, and Oldham, found numerous reasons for delay. Of course, as time went by, it got more and more difficult for The Stones to plunge into filming, if only because this was another area which The Beatles had conquered with their customary flair and efficiency. The Stones were unwilling to come off second-best in that medium as well.

Back in the spring, it had been announced that the group would begin work on their first full-length feature film on April 10. At that point, the film's title was *Back, Behind And In Front*, and Oldham was credited with the original idea. It is doubtful whether this concept was ever very far advanced, however, and the following month it was announced that the rights to a novel called *Only Lovers Left Alice* had been acquired on behalf of the group. The book, by Dave Willis, concerned a teenage takeover of the country and, said Oldham, "could have been written for The Stones". This view was immediately challenged by the author's wife who averred that, on the contrary, The Stones would violate the integrity of the work. She needn't have worried. Though the group continued to refer to the project for the rest of the year, nothing ever got underway. Plans were continually announced – at one point it was even suggested that shooting would start at Shepperton Studios in October – but were never brought to fruition. Part of the problem was that the book the Stones camp had always earnestly wanted was Anthony Burgess' *A Clockwork Orange*, which Jagger, Richard and Oldham in particular had found fascinating. Oldham took his middle name, 'Loog', from the language of the book. Further, he kept dropping hints that The Stones would be filming it. He had been working, he said, on the principle that if you lied often enough it became a reality. It was a precept that had served him well during the group's early years. On this occasion, it didn't work, because Stanley Kubrick had already shrewdly picked up the rights and, although he didn't make the film for some time, (he was hard at work on *2001 – A Space Odyssey*) he was keenly aware of the potential of the project and wasn't prepared to allow the rights to be snatched by some upstart rock 'n' roll group.

Only Lovers Left Alice had therefore become a very poor substitute for the Burgess work, despite the fanfare The Stones' press office gave it. No-one felt strongly enough about it to see it through.

The whole film idea had been too long in gestation. By the time The Stones would have been able to begin work on it, at the close of the UK tour with Ike & Tina Turner, they were simply too exhausted to contemplate the beginning of another arduous project. They were even invited by Brigitte Bardot to appear with her in *Two Weeks In September*, but declined the offer. (They'd met both Bardot and the exceedingly popular French singer Francoise Hardy backstage after their spring concerts in Paris.) They all remained eager to work in films, but somehow they'd missed the boat. Jagger was the one most interested in turning to the cinema, and he was briefly able to embark on a solo career; meanwhile, The Stones' film plans, having been shelved so many times, eventually coalesced into an idea for a TV show. That was to prove equally frustrating.

Life sometimes seems to relish its ironies, and certainly The Stones were wholly unprepared for the course which events took in 1967. Having spent three years of madness on the road, being engaged almost continuously in touring and recording, The Stones looked forward to rest and relaxation; to being able to enjoy a period of leisure, and to be able to appreciate the expensive homes they had all bought. Most of all, they looked forward to a time of peace and quiet, when they could get away from the pressures of living in the public eye. They wanted to fade into the background for a period, forget they were Rolling Stones and recover from the extraordinary strains of the past three years.

Rarely has actuality so completely overturned expectation.

As usual, The Stones themselves invited hostility from the establishment. Just when it seemed that the flames of antagonism had finally died down, they couldn't help affronting a few more sensibilities, and invited a further ordeal-by-Fleet Street that had far more serious ramifications than anything they had previously had to deal with.

Their new year single was titled *Let's Spend The Night Together*, an innocuous enough title for the eighties, but one which flushed out isolated pockets of outraged morality in 1967. Those who objected were clearly out of step with contemporary social mores, and not even the BBC baulked at playing the record. However, certain of those isolated pockets were not without influence.

In America, it was a different story. The song seemed positively amoral, and radio stations across the country tended to bleep out the title, or part of it. The Stones had to reach an accomodation with Ed Sullivan before another promotional appearance on his show was sanctioned. Jagger agreed to change the words to "Let's Spend Some Time Together"; on the TV recording he could be seen mouthing them with the utmost reluctance. Nevertheless, the controversy over the song was not of vast importance, for it had already been agreed to switch sides for the US market, and *Ruby Tuesday* was the top side there.

There are several interesting aspects of the record itself. The first is that it marked the beginning of The Stones' tradition of double-A sided singles. Previously, the B-side may have offered very good value for money, but it had always remained indisputably the B-side. From now on they began to think in terms of double A-sides.

Secondly, the mood of the single is very different. It is a lot calmer. *Ruby Tuesday* is as romantic a song as they have ever composed. There are two reasons for this. The first is that *Have You Seen Your Mother, Baby* had actually taken their previous string of 45s to a crescendo, and now they needed to start off again in a fresh direction. The other reason was offered by Jagger himself. Many of their previous singles had been composed in America, and therefore the slightly jangling, disorientating themes were a result of Jagger's response to living in that slightly crazed, neurotic society; back in the UK, things were more pacific, and thus the songs reflected this. Jagger was responding in a creative way to the environment in which he found himself.

The final points to make are that the single didn't quite reach Number One, and that *Ruby Tuesday* was given an excellent treatment by Melanie in 1970. She took the song to the Top Ten on both sides of the Atlantic. These days, Melanie is hardly a name to conjure with, but her version does not deserve to be underestimated.

The Stones' singles, whatever their changes in character, remained on the same plateau as regards quality; their career as album artists, however, suddenly became astonishingly mercurial. *Between The Buttons* was released on January 20. To this day, no-one has offered a satisfactory explanation as to why this should have been such a terrible album. It is patently clear that both Jagger and Richard were drained of creativity and inspiration, and that they composed the material at a psychologically inadvisable time – i.e. after an extremely arduous schedule, when this was the last task in front of them before they were able to take an extended holiday.

Even that, however, does not explain the wild changes in mood and style to which this album is subject. Some have tried to attribute this to Oldham's overbearing influence, but there are two massive holes in this theory. Why should he have been more, or less, influential on this album than the previous one – the acknowledged masterpiece, *Aftermath?* And in any case it is almost unimaginable that strong personalities like Jagger and Richard, both of whom had extraordinary studio expertise of their own, would have allowed such a situation to develop.

Neither is Brian Jones to blame. He was laid out on the floor much of the time, testimony to the folly of overindulgence in drugs or alcohol. The others would patiently do nothing other than musical doodlings, until he staggered to his feet, made his excuses and left.

No, Jagger and Richard simply cannot slough off responsibility. It is their album, and their failure. Perhaps the reason is that they deliberately tried to broaden their range as songwriters, to master a variety of styles as Lennon and McCartney clearly had. This album bears witness to their inadequacies as all-round songwriting craftsmen.

This certainly seems the most logical explanation, for what is most immediately apparent about the album is its derivativeness. Had this group just been starting out, they wouldn't have got very far.

One track, *Who's Been Sleeping Here* is quite effective until you realise how much it owes to Bob Dylan in general (there is even a burst of Dylan-style harmonica) and to his *Desolation Row* in particular. The tracks which close each side, *Cool, Calm And Collected* and *Something Happened To Me Yesterday* are pure Ray Davies vaudeville – the sort of quasi-Temperance Seven twenties style crossed with English music hall. Even the lyrics on the latter are an embarrassment.

Please Go Home, with its maraccas and Bo Diddley beat, is even derivative of their own early days: astonishing.

Basically, it's an album of filler material, completely lacking the toughness and bite that one already expected of Stones material. Saving graces are rare, though the attempts to introduce some instrumental variety, and to showcase each group member, were worthy enough. There are some commendable drum-sounds on *My Obsession*, and *Connection* is a reasonable track, which is interesting because it's sung by Keith Richard.

Two other tracks, *Yesterday's Papers* and *Back Street Girl* also sound excellent, but the lyrics are thoroughly distasteful. *Yesterday's Papers* resumes the *Out Of Time* theme (and, to strengthen the link between the two, Chris Farlowe covered it to follow up *Out Of Time*, though it had only marginal success). *Back Street Girl* is simply nasty, one of the most reprehensible songs even Jagger has ever written. The Back Street Girl in question (prostitute, mistress) is literally a chattel in this case, as she is told in no uncertain terms that she's to play no part in the singer's own life. The fact that such unpleasant lyrics are incorporated into such an attractive waltz-time tune, to which Brian Jones adds some subtle accordion touches, does not provide a level of irony, only of schizophrenia.

In their last public engagement before the storm broke, The Stones appeared on *Sunday Night at the London Palladium*. Previously the group had staunchly resisted the producer's blandishments, and it was obviously a mistake for them finally to have capitulated. However unwilling they had been to accept the engagement, once they had done so they should have carried it through in good faith; after all, they were themselves using the situation to their own advantage – they had a new single and album to plug, and there was no better nationwide exposure than this. The bill was even a favourable one for them, since Peter Cook and Dudley Moore also starred in that edition. But, having given their performance, The Stones refused to join in the roundabout ride that traditionally closed the show.

Was that a significant dereliction of duty? Actually, yes. The whole procedure was as much a part of the traditional English Sunday as roast beef, and deliberately to offend the sensibilities of the viewing millions was simply discourteous. The show was unadulterated family entertainment; The Stones knew as much – and that was why they had refused invitations for so long. Having agreed, finally, to join in the game and accept the exposure, they should have played by the rules.

Such incidents actually are important. If The Stones wish to preach a new code of morality, fine; certain sections of the population will at least respect their principles, without necessarily endorsing them. Here the matter was entirely different. The whole point is that it was completely unimportant and would therefore have cost The Stones nothing in lost pride,

would have betrayed no precious principles. As a result they seemed to be merely bad-mannered. It was the sort of gormless rebellion The Sex Pistols would later build a career on. A photograph has survived of Oldham engaged in a furious backstage row with Jagger, unavailingly trying to persuade him to do his bit.

Once again, there was a storm of bad publicity. Perhaps this last gesture, this two-fingers to the common folk of old England, actually cost The Stones more than all their other anti-establishment posturings put together.

The Rolling Stones were no more immune than other groups from the fact that it was now 1967. The whole atmosphere of the country was changing, and although in interviews Jagger always tried to maintain his distance from the flower-power philosophy, The Stones could not help being caught up in the mood of the times. Jagger's clothes, and those of the rest of the group, became more colourful and effeminate.

The essential element in this developing sub-culture was, of course, the increasing use of drugs. That was the factor which distinguished this particular phase of adolescent fashion from any other and which, as far as the guardians of the status quo were concerned, made it that much more threatening.

On February 5 one of those salacious exposé stories – nauseating journalism – appeared in the *News of the World*. The article adumbrated the ways in which drugs were becoming an increasingly important part of the pop scene. Although the group which featured most prominently in the feature was the Moody Blues, The Stones almost inevitably came under fire as well, and there were several quotes from Mick Jagger about the attractions of experimenting with drugs.

In fact, these quotes had been obtained several months earlier, and the Stone who had been holding forth on the subject was not Jagger at all, but Brian Jones. Therefore when Jagger, once again appearing on the *Eamonn Andrews Show*, was asked that same evening for his opinion of the piece, he replied that he would be suing the paper for libel; and indeed a writ from his solicitors to this effect soon arrived at the *News of the World* offices.

All this is very important. The *NoW* had clearly boobed; Jagger's claim for damages could have been substantial. The *NoW* therefore responded in a vindictive manner. The paper hired detectives to shadow both Jagger and Richard during the course of the following week, and the next Sunday the paper made its move, tipping off the local constabulary that illicit goings-on were in progress at Richard's Sussex retreat, Redlands. Fifteen policemen and women raided the guitarist's West Wittering home, where a party was apparently in progress, although festivities must have been slightly dampened by the fact that there was only one girl present – Marianne Faithfull – amongst eight male guests. Marianne was doing sterling work to compensate for this imbalance, however, and at the time of the raid was found to be naked.

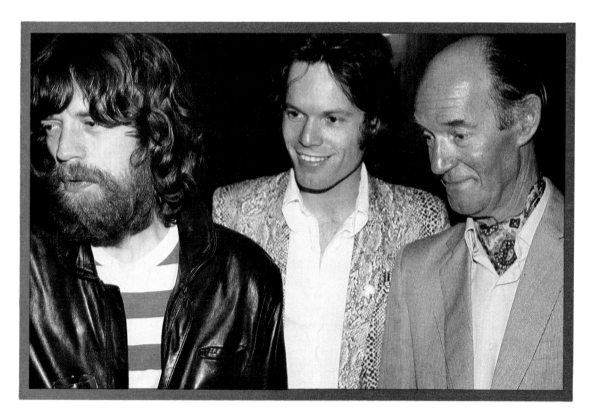

Most of the assembled party had been tripping on acid all day, so they were hardly capable of dealing with this unwelcome – but not, if you'll pardon the pun, un-warranted – intrusion. Three people were subsequently charged under Dangerous Drugs legislation. The fact that two of these were Jagger and Richard suggests that they had been the main targets of the raid; the other was the art gallery owner, Robert Fraser.

While Fraser then returned to London, the others stayed in Sussex. No charges were brought immediately after the raid – certain substances were simply taken away to be analysed. Hence, the others were left in a state of suspended animation. Their immediate reaction was to get out of the country for a while, to remove themselves from a claustrophobic situation.

They decided to go to Morocco. Keith set off in his Bentley, with Brian and Anita and a chauffeur. It was arranged that Mick and Marianne, and Robert Fraser and Christopher Gibbs, the nephew of the former governor of the country then still known as Rhodesia, would meet them in Tangier.

It was a particularly eventful trip. Jones got ill en route and was hospitalised in Toulon, in France. After this Richard and Anita Pallenberg began to enjoy each other's company. Jones became increasingly distraught about the situation, and, once he'd rejoined the others, it became increasingly difficult to deal with; it is hard not to feel some sympathy for him, although he did attack Anita violently on at least one occasion. Finally, with the entire company in Marrakesh, Keith and Anita fled, first of all to Tangier and then back to London.

Brian's affair with Anita had come to an end, causing an acceleration in the pace of decline of his physical and emotional well-being. One of his last personal triumphs was to compose the music for a German film, A Degree Of Murder, in which Anita had a starring role. He'd relished the opportunity to work alone, and was ready to respond to the faith that had been placed in him. His soundtrack music covered a range of styles, and was performed on a variety of instruments – he'd personally played piano, sitar, dulcimer, harmonica, organ and autoharp.

The director pronounced himself well satisfied with Brian's work. He was Volker Schlondorff, who'd made his name the previous year with Young Torless, but whose hour of greatest triumph – an Academy Award – arrived much later, in 1980, with The Tin Drum. A Degree Of Murder was shown at the Cannes Film Festival; it was at that time that Brian made a last, despairing attempt to win back Anita.

The Moroccan trip wasn't the only escape from the drugs problems that were confronting Jagger and Richard. The group also had a three-week continental tour, the only dates booked for them during 1967, to complete during March and April.

Naturally, the publicity about the West Wittering raid had preceded them, and the whole trip became

most uncomfortable, since The Stones were frequently subjected to rigorous and humiliating searches at airports. The tone was set in Oerbro, Sweden, at the very start of the tour.

The dates were noted for the usual scenes of high excitement which frequently overflowed to mass hysteria and violence. There were several incidents in Sweden, and after a number of gigs fans and policemen required hospital treatment. In Halsingborg, fans threw bottles, chairs and fireworks on to the stage, and police retaliated with truncheons and dogs. Jagger once again protested about the over-reactions of the authorities.

There were problems in Vienna when The Stones played the town hall, a venue that seated fourteen thousand. After someone had thrown a smoke-bomb on to the stage, serious fighting developed between police and fans. There were a number of casualties, and one hundred and fifty-four arrests were made. Subsequently, Stones' concerts in Milan caused difficulties, and when the group returned to the Paris Olympia there were actually riots in the street outside the theatre.

Towards the end of the tour, The Stones played one date in East Europe, in Warsaw. While there was general uproar inside the Palace of Culture, outside the venue about twelve thousand disappointed fans without tickets were expressing their disappointment violently, and a full-scale riot developed. The police only succeeded in restoring control by bringing in armoured cars and using water hoses. The main complaint of those outside had been that ticket distribution had not been conducted fairly, but that tickets had gone to party officials and to specially-approved people.

The Stones returned home, stopping off in Zurich for one last concert before twelve thousand fans. Inevitably, there was pandemonium almost from the beginning of the show.

Within a month of their return to Britain, the group knew they were under severe pressure. Mick was charged with possession of pep pills and Keith with permitting his house to be used for the smoking of hashish. On the very day that they were remanded on bail, prior to being tried at West Sussex Quarter Sessions, Brian Jones was arrested at his flat in Courtfield Road, and charged with the possession of Indian hemp. For The Stones, the pleasures of being able to spend the summer at home in England had turned very sour, and the period became an immense strain for them all. Richard, in fact, left the country again and spent the summer months living with Anita in Rome, where she was filming Roger Vadim's Barbarella with Jane Fonda. He returned only to sort out legal matters or to attend recording sessions. The trial of Jagger and Richard opened in Chichester on June 22 before Judge Block. Much of the trial seemed to turn on the strange behaviour of Marianne Faithfull (referred to only as 'Miss X' during the trial, though the entire country seemed fully aware of her identity), whose

naked presence amongst an otherwise entirely male company was held to be sufficient evidence of the depravity of the occasion. The prosecution omitted to mention that such behaviour was not in itself illegal, and the revelations helped to fuel a fresh wave of animosity to the group. In retrospect, it was a big mistake to have tried to conceal Marianne's identity (The Stones had wanted to ensure that no damage was done to her career) since the references to her as 'Miss X' only made events seem more lurid.

Jagger's pep pills had been legally purchased in Italy, and, further, his doctor agreed that he would have given a prescription for them, had he needed one. The charge, therefore, was a technical one. In Richard's case, the charge was a vague one, for which the prosecution had to rely entirely on tenuous evidence. Richard's solicitor was the Q.C. Mr. Michael Havers. Today, he is Sir Michael Havers, and the Conservative administration's Attorney-General.

It was impossible to escape the conclusion that the trial was virtually rigged, and indeed Jagger had been privately warned that the legal profession was out to get the group. All three were found guilty. Keith was sentenced to twelve months' imprisonment, Jagger got three months and Fraser six months. They were then all released on bail, pending their appeal.

The severity of the sentences acted in The Stones' favour. Public sympathy swung towards them, and there was a growing feeling that, although society had wanted to make examples of The Stones, this was really excessive. After all, even then it was uncommon for first offenders facing such charges to be given harsh prison sentences.

It was nevertheless a greatly distressing period for Jagger and Richard. Two youths were arrested in a demonstration by Stones' fans outside the *News of the World* offices; and Christopher Gibbs, who admitted that he had been one of those at the party, protested about the punishment: "If anyone was smoking Indian hemp, I was not aware of it. It was just an ordinary weekend by the sea." The Who issued a tribute disc, pairing two Jagger-Richard compositions, *Under My Thumb* and *The Last Time*, and announced that royalties would be donated towards The Stones' defence costs.

As it happened, though, the most telling support of all came from the wholly unlikely direction of *The Times*. In a famous editorial, entitled 'Who Breaks a Butterfly on a Wheel?', the then-editor, William Rees-Mogg (now Sir William, and chairman of the Arts Council) argued that the evidence against Richard was purely circumstantial, and pointed out that Jagger's offence was a technical one, which even someone like the Archbishop of Canterbury could unwittingly have committed. It was therefore clear that the two Stones had been denied normal British justice. It was an extremely influential leader, and there was little surprise – but greater relief, nonetheless – when the Appeal Court dealt differently with the cases at the end of July. Richard's conviction was quashed. The Appeal Judges ruled that Judge Block had mis-directed the jury and allowed them to be influenced by the behaviour of Miss X which was, in strictly legal terms, entirely irrelevant. Jagger's conviction was allowed to stand, but the sentence was set aside and he was given a conditional discharge.

There was one sad aspect of the case. The six-month sentence of Robert Fraser stood. After all, he'd been convicted of possession of heroin, and has later admitted that he was an addict at the time. However, he got the worst of both worlds. Because of his association with The Stones, he'd been harshly treated at the original trial. Yet in the appeal they were able to turn their celebrity to advantage – but this didn't benefit him. Thus, he had suffered the disadvantages in the first place without being able to avail himself of the advantages in the second. He served his sentence.

At a press conference afterwards, which he gave with Marianne, Jagger admitted that he had mentally and physically prepared himself for going to prison, but that it was lovely to be free again. The whole experience seemed to have an unsettling effect on him.

Although he had won in the end, he was really soured by the episode, which after all had taken up nearly six months of his life at a most important time in the history of The Stones. He agreed that the bust had adversely affected the development of the group, by preventing them from concentrating properly on their work in the recording studio as they had intended to do, and the sessions for the next album became impossibly attenuated.

The successful appeal was marked in two ways. First of all, Jagger appeared in a discussion programme about contemporary social values with authorities like Rees-Mogg and Dr. John Robinson, the author of *Honest To God*. Then, the group rushed into the studios to complete their next single – *We Love You*, which thus became their first wholly made-in-Britain release for over three years. This took the place of *English Summer*, the song that had been earmarked for release, but which has never been issued.

The song opened, famously, with Brian Jones providing a Phantom-of-the-Opera atmosphere on mellotron, and then the sounds of chains, footsteps echoing hollowly along a corridor and the sound of a cell-door slamming. The record then developed into *We Love You*, a feeling aimed genuinely at the fans who had supported them, and sarcastically at the authorities who had done their damnedest to incarcerate them.

By then the summer of love, in which Jagger and Richard had played their ironic part, was well under way. Jones, who had lately returned from the famed Monterey Pop Festival had seen it all for himself in America. The *We Love You* single was thus a highly topical, genuinely interesting artefact of its time. John Lennon and Paul McCartney are popularly supposed to have been at the sessions, joining in on the chorus, though no-one has ever been able either to confirm or deny this. It's probably true, though, especially since it precisely mirrors events at the beginning of the month when Mick and Marianne had been among those heard (and seen) singing with The Beatles on *All You Need Is Love*.

We Love You was coupled with *Dandelion*, which had been recorded with *Ruby Tuesday* the previous November, but now seemed a particularly apposite release, since its summery, nursery rhyme flavour caught the mood of the time. The record's release was assisted by an extravagant promotional film, in which Mick, Marianne and Keith did their own version of *The Trials of Oscar Wilde*, a further indication that Jagger still believed that the establishment made him a martyr for his art. It was, however, hardly appropriate to invoke a *cause célèbre* like the Wilde case; after all, the latter had served a prison sentence – Jagger had, ultimately, been let off.

For Jones, meanwhile, the year was an intensely wearing one. He had been placed under intense emotional strain, both through the rupture of his relationship with Anita, and through the drugs charge that had been brought against him. Since his health had been delicate to begin with – he suffered badly from asthma – it was no real shock when he was hospitalised on July 6 suffering from strain. After holidaying in Marbella, Spain, and his visit to Monterey, he had returned to London for the recording of *We Love You*, but was only intermittently able to participate in the sessions for the next albums, and would frequently make apologies for absence. (The final album, nevertheless, bore clear evidence of his creative contributions.) In the meantime, the others got on without him. He became increasingly apprehensive about his forthcoming trial.

In the event, on October 30, Jones pleaded guilty to possession of Indian hemp and to allowing his flat to be used for the smoking of the drug. He was sentenced to nine months' imprisonment – once again, a severe and exemplary custodial term. The following day he was released on bail, pending appeal. At the same time, there was a protest march down King's Road, Chelsea; Mick's brother Chris was one of those arrested and charged with obstructing the police.

Thereafter, Jones' cause was assisted by some extraordinary remarks made by Judge Block at, of all places, the Horsham Ploughing and Agricultural Society dinner. With an embarrassing lack of wit, Block had allowed his speech about farming to move on to the subject of "stones": "we did our best to cut those Stones down to size, but alas it was not to be." The remarks were completely tactless. They were singularly opportune as far as Jones was concerned, for, as the late Leslie Perrin, the group's diligent press officer, was quick to seize upon, they covered ground which was *sub judice*, since the Jones' appeal was still to be heard. It was thus the Judge who was cut down to size, and the legal establishment that was made to look inept. On December 13, the appeal court duly set aside Jones' sentence.

He had also been assisted by the evidence of three psychiatrists, who all discovered symptoms of considerable mental strain. One described him as "an extremely frightened young man". Jones was obliged to make a rather grovelling statement, confirming establishment prejudices about the dangers of drug-taking. Despite Jones' growing estrangement from the rest of the group, Jagger was in court throughout the three-day hearing.

Despite the happy outcome, though, the emotional strain had been considerable, and Jones' condition had deteriorated. Just two days later, he was hospitalised again.

The summer had been marked by one change of great significance in The Stones' camp: Oldham had been jettisoned. His gambits had always been founded on pure bluff, and it now seemed as though The Stones no longer needed that kind of treatment. Oldham had done his job – he was not of any particular use to them any more. He had established The Stones, but now he was becoming an embarrassment. The Stones did not need his sub-Spector musical fantasies, and although

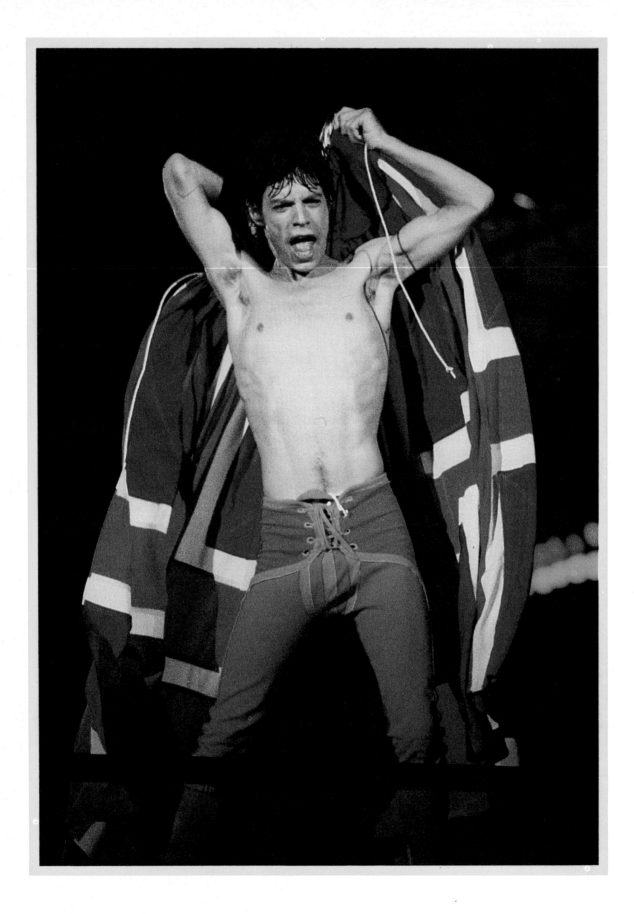

he'd always been credited as producer, he'd tended to get through that task too largely by bluff. Obviously, Jagger and Richard would by now have been capable of producing the material themselves. The row backstage at the *Sunday Night at the London Palladium* show was one of the last occasions on which Oldham was acting literally as the group's manager – and then Jagger had paid no attention to him.

There wasn't a major bust-up. The Stones simply made it clear that they no longer needed him around, and apparently on album sessions that summer they simply stood around playing conventional blues material, poorly, until Oldham got up and left, never to return. Perhaps Jagger and Richard blamed him for the *Between The Buttons* fiasco. As has been indicated, it would have been self-deception if they did; but they were quite capable of that.

In a way, The Stones had used up Oldham. He had nothing more to contribute, no useful services to perform, and so they got rid of him. Nevertheless they had far more reason to be grateful to him than they perhaps admitted to themselves.

In the beginning, it was Oldham who recognised the crucial fact that everything really did revolve around The Beatles. What he did therefore was to create this syzygy, in which The Stones appeared as the under-side of The Beatles; white and black, sun and moon, heaven and hell, whatever. The Rolling Stones thereby stood in relation to The Beatles, they had a perspective beside them. No other group did. Other groups were simply below The Beatles.

All the Stones went to New York in September. Jagger and Richard initially had difficulty getting in, until the final outcome of their court cases was made clear. This was the only time they visited the States as a group during the year, and it was announced that the purpose of their visit was to have business talks with Allan Klein. It quickly became clear, of course, that what was actually being discussed was how to manoeuvre Oldham out of the picture.

Klein himself would hardly have been a passive party in the rift; that wasn't in his nature. It suited him to have Oldham out of the way; he had achieved his ambition of becoming sole manager of the group. It is reasonable to suppose that he had twisted the knife in Oldham's back, and had been slyly undermining the latter's standing with the group whenever the opportunity arose.

So, events turned in Klein's favour, and on September 30 there was a curt announcement from The Rolling Stones press office: the partnership between Oldham and The Stones had been dissolved.

In the midst of all these legal and administrative wranglings, The Stones could have been excused for paying only cursory attention to the summer of love. Jagger, characteristically, resisted making statements that either endorsed or condemned it, but lent just enough of his support to the contemporary scene so that he and Marianne were automatically numbered among the beautiful people – but did not go overboard

in case they looked foolish afterwards. Throughout the year he had taken to wearing paisley or flowered jackets and shirts. At the end of August, he and Marianne, kaftanned á la mode, set off to Bangor to join The Beatles in the weekend of genuflection at the feet of the Maharishi Mahesh Yogi. The Beatles had to flee to London after hearing of the death of their manager, Brian Epstein, but they vowed to return. Mick and Marianne had by then had enough anyway; they vowed never to return.

Nevertheless, Jagger, with more opportunity at this time for reading, had been absorbing books concerning mysticism, the supernatural and Chinese philosophy – all themes which guided him during the preparation of the group's next album.

This was recorded at a snail's pace throughout the year, having been interrupted by all manner of difficulties, though notably the bust-up with Oldham (it was obviously difficult to proceed when he was ostensibly in charge of proceedings) and the drugs trials, which preoccupied at least one member of the group right throughout the year from February to December. Even if Brian Jones was by then hardly a group member any longer, his fate was still of concern to them (as Jagger's presence at his appeal indicates).

The other huge obstacle which inhibited their recording plans was the release of The Beatles' *Sergeant Pepper's Lonely Hearts Club Band*. There are many who still consider it to be the outstanding rock album of all time. Certainly its contemporary impact was measured seismographically. If anything, it was received with more respect from The Beatles' fellow-artists than affection from the public (though this is a moot point). Certainly, there were many performers who felt their own stature belittled by it. None more so than Brian Wilson, of The Beach Boys, who abandoned in despair the work on which he was engaged. The Beach Boys had been the main American rivals to The Beatles, and Wilson felt he could no longer compete.

Similarly, Jagger was taken aback by the sheer quality of *Sergeant Pepper*, but he refused to be overawed. He determined that The Stones should respond on equal terms to the masterpieces. It was an ambition doomed to failure, but Jagger should at least be given credit for taking up the cudgels.

Their Satanic Majesties Request was released in December 1967. If it was not quite greeted with howls of derisory laughter, it was certainly given a lukewarm reception.

Undoubtedly The Stones' initial mistake was trying to emulate the audacious inventiveness of the *Pepper* cover. *Satanic Majesties* had an extremely expensive 3-D inset on the sleeve (that today adds three pounds to the price of the record). The style of the photograph too was reminiscent of *Sergeant Pepper*; to cap it all, The Stones had even hidden the faces of the four Beatles amongst the greenery either side of the group; there had been allegations for over three years that The

Stones always looked to The Beatles for their ideas, and the cover of the new album apparently offered conclusive proof of that. There were many who'd dismissed the album even before they'd reached the music.

In fact, the music was of variable quality. The original idea – of making the album as a psychedelic satire on the Queen – had come to Jagger the day after the release of *Sergeant Pepper*, but the theme was not convincingly carried through on the album. It was too much of a hotch-potch. After the break with Oldham, Jagger and Richard became carried away with the potential of the recording studio (and, in this too, they were clearly influenced by the example of The Beatles, and the exciting production-work on *Sergeant Pepper*), and thus the tracks tend to be over-elaborate. The standard of composition too was inconsistent, although some tracks hardly qualified as 'songs', but were just a few disjointed ideas strung together. In this respect, the contributions of Brian Jones had been influential, particularly with respect to the use of electronics, pre-recorded tapes and Moroccan tribal music.

The whole project was always just a bit too ambitious, and hovering just outside the group's control. It is nevertheless infinitely more interesting and worthwhile than *Between The Buttons*, and it contains two tracks of great quality – *She's A Rainbow* and *2000 Light Years From Home*. It was only when

these tracks were later included on the group's second hits compilation that their excellence became more generally appreciated.

The album also featured a Bill Wyman track, *In Another Land*, recorded with Charlie Watts, Nicky Hopkins and Steve Mariott; he thus became the first of the other three Stones to break the Jagger-Richard duopoly.

The album was, in commercial as well as aesthetic terms, a comparative failure, though its late release, uncomfortably close to Christmas, partly accounted for that.

So The Stones were temporarily deflated – though it would not be long before a powerful personality like Jagger bounced back. Meanwhile, the group announced that they were forming their own Mother Earth record label. Earlier in the year Jagger had been engaged in discussions with Paul McCartney about the feasibility of the two groups forming their own company together – but a union of that sort never came close to fruition. While The Beatles' own ill-fated Apple was launched in 1968, The Stones were the first to make their intentions public. Mother Earth was their label, and Marianne Faithfull was its first signing. Needless to say, this was merely another of those grandiose schemes that came to nothing. There were a lot of them about in 1967.

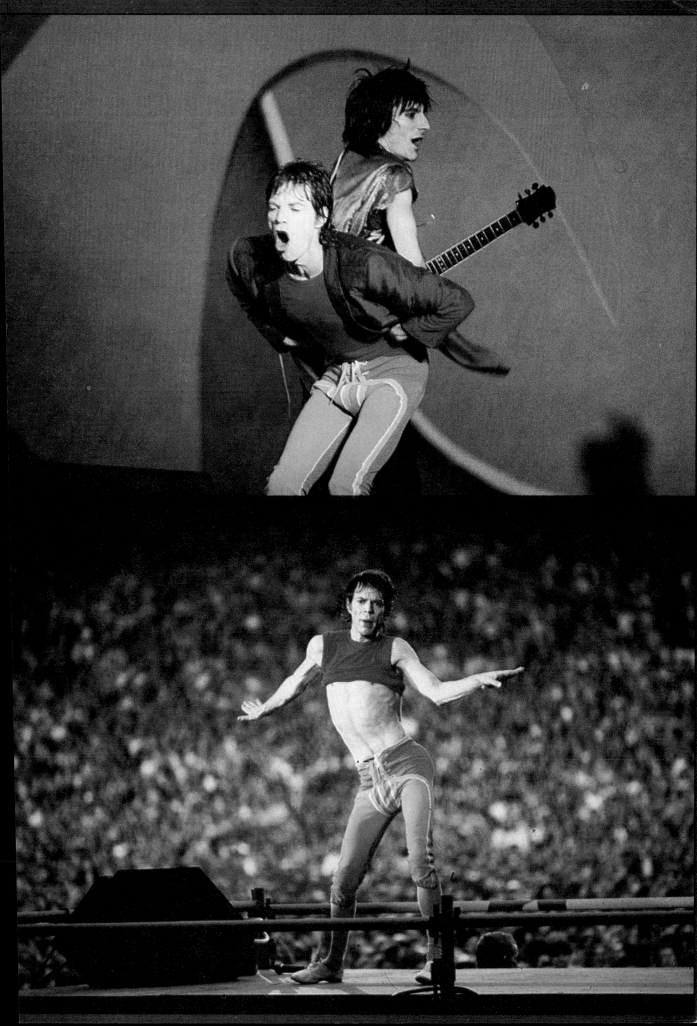

7

By 1968 it was clear to Jagger and the others that the decision to run down their hectic schedule had brought no relief; they had simply exchanged old pressures for new ones. They remained the *bêtes noires* of British society, hounded at regular intervals. Furthermore, the recording career, which the abandonment of touring had been designed to stimulate, had actually foundered. Both the last album (*Satanic Majesties*) and the last single (*We Love You*) had been accorded only lukewarm receptions. This may have been unjust – the latent qualities of the album were not generally recognised, and *We Love You* was actually an extremely fine single, albeit an untypical one. These factors weren't sufficient compensation for Jagger, however. He was determined that The Stones should quickly become a name to be reckoned with again.

Two immediate decisions were taken. The group would abandon the *avant-garde* direction that *Satanic Majesties* had taken, and return to the blues – and R&B-based style of the group's most effective material. Secondly, it was decided to call in a producer, since their efforts at self-production had not been conspicuously successful. They chose Jimmy Miller, an independent producer previously known for his work with acts on Chris Blackwell's Island label, and in particular The Spencer Davis Group. His work on *Gimme Some Lovin'* and *I'm A Man*, the band's last two major hits, was noted for its verve. Miller, of course, didn't need time to think over Jagger's offer; he was tingling with excitement straight away.

Beggar's Banquet was thus virtually the work of Jagger, Richard and Miller. Richard would go over to Jagger's London flat – first of all in Chester Square, and then in Cheyne Walk – and the two would compose material together, on acoustic guitars, before inviting Miller in to discuss how the song should be developed; or, perhaps, they might all three go down to Redlands to work on material there. Miller was naturally conscious that he was on trial, and it must have been difficult for him to make contributions without appearing either too forceful or insufficiently imaginative. He nevertheless came through with flying colours. Jagger was particularly impressed by the fact that "he does not have an ego problem"; this naturally placed him in complete contrast to the two producers the group had previously been associated with.

The material for the album was recorded during the spring months at Olympic Studios, with Glyn Johns acting as engineer. Jagger and Richard tended to work unstintingly once they had embarked on a project (the *Satanic Majesties* sessions being an obvious, and understandable, exception) but the pace was slightly more relaxed than it had been previously. For a start, they could now afford the time, and also they were determined to make sure that there were no slip-ups.

Because the album was taking longer than they'd originally planned, they issued a single in advance of it. *Jumpin' Jack Flash* was released on May 24, 1968. After the mishaps of the previous year, this testified to a new virility. It was extraordinarily powerful, right from the heavy Richard guitar chords that opened the song, and almost marked a synthesis of The Stones' career to date. While the sound itself reached back across the years to the urgent R&B of their beginnings, the lyrics echoed the group's most recent theme – satanic majesties. Indeed, the song would have been more thematically apposite on that last album than any of the tracks that were actually on it.

Jumpin' Jack Flash put Jagger in his element. He was able to inject a high level of threatening intent into the vocals, he was able to prance on stage in a particularly minatory way. It was perfect for him, and equally it couldn't have worked for any other vocalist. One might note, parenthetically, that in this respect The Beatles and The Stones were binary opposites: the faith The Beatles almost invariably put in the melody meant that their songs provided ideal source material for other artists; virtually everything The Stones have done, however, has been so idiosyncratic that no-one else has been able to cover it. Having said that, *Jumpin' Jack Flash* itself was covered in memorable circumstances – for Leon Russell performed the song at the Concert for Bangla Desh in 1971.

The song sounded sensational, and much of that can be attributed to Jimmy Miller who conclusively showed that The Stones had no need to do their recording in the States. Certainly, it had a sensational impact, and quickly topped the charts the world over. In a way, it had been a gamble to bring in a new producer at a time when the group's record success seemed to be ebbing. Straight away, however, it had proved the shrewdest of moves. Mick Jagger's relief that all had gone so well was almost palpable.

Since it had been such an important release for the group, they had accordingly given it some useful pre-publicity by making an unscheduled appearance at the 1968 NME Pollwinners' Concert. Although it was only two years since their previous appearance at this event, The Stones had been through the hurricane in the interim. So, they appeared on their own initiative, simply to test out the water again. They performed only two songs – *Satisfaction* being the other – but it was enough. They had restored their confidence in themselves, and rediscovered their *raison d' être*, by performing live to a home audience for the first time in eighteen months; and they had introduced *Jumpin' Jack Flash*, the stone on which their career would be re-built.

The promotional film used with *Jumpin' Jack Flash* was also important. It showed the band actually performing the song (thus bucking the bucolic trend that was developing to show groups disporting themselves in sundry sun-speckled settings) – the ideal format since it allowed Jagger, showman that he is, to convey the power and ferocious energy of the song. Also, The Stones all appeared wearing make-up – Jagger, naturally, making himself appear particularly saturnine. Such a crude device could have sunk the careers of some groups, but they made it work – simply because it was just another element which helped to make the film itself so memorably vivid. Years later, this androgynous gesture was seen as the precursor of an entire rock genre.

Although The Stones as a group were resurgent, individually only four of them felt the adrenalin flowing again. Brian Jones, inevitably, was the exception. By this time, he was becoming seriously ill. He clearly hadn't been able to withstand the psychological strains imposed upon him. The others knew that he was in no condition to tour, and furthermore had no wish to embarrass him even by asking him to undertake a series of dates. That is why it had been decided to arrange a one-off performance.

However, on May 21, Jones was busted again, when police raided his King's Road flat, found Brian on the floor telephoning the group's personal assistant, and proceeded to charge him with possession of cannabis. He was sent for trial on June 11.

This new source of tension in Jones' life occurred at the moment when the group were actually, finally, making their first film. They were appearing in *One Plus One*, the work of the French *avant-garde* director, Jean-Luc Godard.

Earlier in the sixties Godard had been one of the most fashionable names of all, but by this time he was losing a little of his clout. Most of the films on which he had built his reputation, from *A Bout de Souffle* to *Alphaville* and the classic *Pierrot Le Fou* had been made by 1965. He did tend to make films rather too quickly – logically, in his view, since he scorned all the tools of the film-makers trade that contributed towards a "professional finish" – and he was also finding it difficult to work further permutations on his central theme of the decadence of Western capitalism.

The Stones, though, were naturally attracted to him, as a genuinely *avant-garde* and anti-establishment director; for Godard it was a welcome opportunity to give his films the extra commercial charge that they were beginning to need. When the cameras arrived at Olympic Studios, The Stones happened to be rehearsing *Sympathy For The Devil*. There could have been no song more suited to Godard's purposes. Administering cultural shocks was his territory as much

as it was The Stones'. He accordingly filmed the group going through the tedious processes of rehearsal to perfect the song.

However, he was never able to integrate these scenes into the rest of the film. Neither do The Stones appear in any other context. The studio scenes are just intercut, in apparently random fashion, with scenes from what was otherwise an unexceptional Godard film. Thus this transitory alliance between two of the anti-heroes of contemporary culture yielded little to either party. The Stones' footage was of minimal interest, and their stature was not enhanced by working with a director whose most creative years were behind him. Neither did Godard benefit. His public was clearly finding his films increasingly unrewarding. The presence of The Stones boosted attendances, of course, (although, to maximise audience potential in this way, Godard's own title was quickly dropped by distributors in favour of *Sympathy For The Devil*), but most of those who went to see The Stones probably came away making a mental note to avoid future Godard movies.

All this lay in the future. At the time of the filming itself, Jagger sensed a new buoyancy in the band's career. The Stones took out ads in the music press to express their gratitude to all those who had put *Jack Flash* at Number One. The message went on: "We are slaving over a hot album which is coming out next month."

Well, not quite. At one time, release was firmly slated for July 26, Jagger's birthday, but for once The Stones missed their deadline, as they aimed for perfection. The success of *Jumpin' Jack Flash* had allayed fears that their recording career might have slipped into irreversible decline and so diminished the sense or urgency regarding the completion of the album.

Nevertheless, it is fascinating that they were so painstaking over this one: they were really determined to get it right this time. At one point, Jagger took a short break in Ireland, and continued writing there, in a less claustrophobic atmosphere. Then in August he flew to the West Coast of America with Jimmy Miller, to complete the mixing in the RCA Studios. Richard, Watts and Marianne Faithfull all flew out to join them.

The album was to be the triumphal outcome of six months' exceptionally hard work. Giant billboards were put up in London, Birmingham and Manchester announcing the imminent arrival of the masterwork. Finally, *Beggar's Banquet* was ready for release.

No, it wasn't. Decca Records objected as strongly as possible to the artwork for the gatefold sleeve. One side was the photograph that had been used on the billboards, showing The Stones enjoying their banquet, in characteristically debauched style. Their other spread was the sensitive one: it simply showed a lavatory wall covered with graffiti. Mick Jagger thought he had anticipated record company sensitivities by not showing the toilet seats, just the cisterns. However, Decca were not appeased. They resolutely refused to

Top: left to right; Dana Gillespie, Mick Ronson, Jeff Beck, David Bowie, Lou Reed, Mick Jagger.

issue the record with that sleeve. Jagger cursed this example of what he deemed to be interfering censorship, and suggested sardonically that the record could be marketed in a brown paper bag with 'Unfit for Children' stamped on the outside. This may have been a genuine attempt at a compromise – but it cut no ice with Decca.

While antlers were locked, the group's US outlet (London Records, Decca's US arm) took one of the tracks held in abeyance, *Street Fightin' Man* and issued it as a single (with another track, *No Expectations* on the B side).

Immediately, another furore broke out. After 1967, and the summer of love, 1968 brought a summer of flaming passions and revolutionary ardour, as the youth of the countries of the West, provoked by, among other things, American involvement in South-East Asia, took to the streets and set about the overthrow of the established order. Though there were protests and demonstrations across America and Europe that summer, the ones which made the strongest impressions were the student riots in Paris in May, which took on some of the aspects of a new French Revolution as General de Gaulle was forced to flee the capital; and the demonstrations in Chicago in August, at the Democratic Convention. Jagger had actually written *Street Fightin' Man* in response to the former. American prejudice against the record was rooted in the thought that it seemed to be a celebration of the latter – an urban guerilla tract no less. Decca obligingly encouraged this viewpoint by issuing the record with a sleeve photograph of rioting in Los Angeles. In the event, many radio stations decided to ban the single, which accordingly fared poorly in the US charts.

In the meantime, the row about the artwork was still on the boil, with neither side yielding an inch. The contentious material is reproduced, the same size as it would have been for the album, on pages 52-3 of Roy Carr's *The Rolling Stones – An Illustrated Record*. It raises more questions than it answers. In particular, it raises the question of what on earth was either side so impassioned about? Rarely can men's toilet graffiti have been so totally devoid of interest; a suggestion that 'God rolls his own' being perhaps the only piece of scribble that might have offended anyone. What was otherwise most noticeable was the misspelling of the album title – *Begger's Banquet*. There was nothing to alarm the record company here; but equally there was nothing of which The Stones needed to be defensive. It was a totally witless idea, and deserved scrapping irrespective of Decca's attitude.

So why did each side become so entrenched? It can only be assumed that Decca imagined that the graffiti *must* be more scurrilous than it appeared to be. Perhaps there was the odd comment that they didn't understand but imagined the worst. The opposition of the company obviously made The Stones more intransigent. To them, it seemed absolutely unexcusable that the company should attempt to interfere in what they saw as the complete creative process involved in making a record. Richard said as much: "The job of the record company is to distribute. All they've got to do is put it in the shops, not dictate to people what they should or should not have."

The fact that there was such a titanic struggle over such a slight matter nevertheless indicated the extent of the gulf between artists and company. It became crystal-clear that The Stones would be moving on once their contract expired.

Nevertheless, the position remained the same: a dispute over some crass artwork impeded the release of an album of magnificent music. Richard had already begun composing material for the *next* album (*Let It Bleed*), and Jagger had embarked on a fresh career.

During those autumn months, he was working hard making *Performance*, the Nicolas Roeg-Donald Cammell film with James Fox. After the years of procrastination, Jagger had suddenly plunged into the icy waters of the film business. Having worked during the summer with one of the living legends of the cinema, it was now he spent the autumn in harness with a tyro director, but one whose career would prove to be equally as controversial as Godard's.

On September 26, Brian Jones was found guilty of the possession of cannabis. After his conviction the previous year (his sentence may have been set aside, but the conviction stood), he was fearing the worst: a punitive prison sentence. This might well have happened, but fortunately for Jones the bust had taken place at his London flat, and the case was therefore to be heard at the Inner London sessions. Magistrates in the metropolis tended to be somewhat more enlightened about drug offences than their country cousins and accordingly, Jones was treated leniently and fined fifty pounds, with one hundred and five pounds costs. Perhaps the judges had taken into account Jones' deteriorating physical condition; perhaps the fact that the defence case was once again put by Michael Havers helped; probably the bench just knew that it was ridiculous that possession of cannabis should have been a criminal offence. So, to their lasting credit, they disregarded the letter of the law.

The fact that the charges had actually been proved, however, meant that Jones now had two separate convictions, and this would undoubtedly have proved a handicap if the band had wanted to tour.

In the meantime, Jones paid the fine, and discovered he had enough money left over to purchase Cotchford Farm in Sussex, the house where A. A. Milne had written *Winnie-the-Pooh*.

At the beginning of November, Jagger was telling reporters that he'd completely lost interest in the fate of *Beggar's Banquet*. By the middle of the month, though, an agreement had been reached; Jagger had simply conceded defeat. The lavatory artwork was dropped altogether, and the record came in a simple cream cover, with an invitation, written in an ironically elegant script, to the banquet. It was released in

December 1968.

Beggar's Banquet was a classic album – different in style from almost everything the group had previously done. The sub-Spector trademarks were jettisoned. There was much to admire in this production, but in a wholly different way. There was no attempt to achieve a total, overall sound. Instead great emphasis was placed on the separation of instruments. Much of the album was acoustic-based, though it was no less powerful for that. The songs were nearly all finely crafted.

Each side began with a stunning track: *Sympathy For The Devil* had a tremendous rhythm, in which the maraccas, The Stones' favourite stand-by, were prominent. Nicky Hopkins' piano was also an important feature of the track. Overall, it was seductively rhythmic. By contrast, *Street Fightin' Man*, which opened side two, was distinguished by its sheer power, courtesy of the guitars, bass and Charlie Watts' drumming.

Nicky Hopkins had been heavily involved with the recording of the album and so, inevitably, had Jack Nitzsche who had flown over to help out. His largest single piece of assistance had been to bring with him an imaginative slide guitarist of rich promise, Ry Cooder.

At that time, virtually everything in the rock business was new to Cooder, and he certainly found The Stones' social scene a little overwhelming. He nevertheless contributed much excellent work to the sessions, as can be heard on tracks such as *No Expectations* and *Prodigal Son* (an old blues by the Rev. Robert Wilkins, the only non-original on the album). *No Expectations* was itself a bluesy, poignant track which offered more conventional song qualities than much of their material, and unsurprisingly did attract cover versions (from Joan Baez, amongst others). *Prodigal Son*, *No Expectations* and *Dear Doctor* also: all these tracks attested to The Stones' blues heritage.

With this kind of prevailing atmosphere, it was fitting that two of the tracks should have embraced a working-class ideology; but *Factory Girl* was another of Jagger's patronising ditties about lower-class girls, who seemed to exist for him only to satisfy debased sexual appetites. *Salt Of The Earth* was a lengthy, rousing finale, with a group of three girl singers and a choir coming in towards the end – in what was the most flamboyant and radical departure from the group's established style – before Nicky Hopkins takes it away on piano.

The song purports to be a tribute to the ordinary folk who toil for no reward: "Let's drink to the hard-working peoples", etc. Some have heard it as a ringing

statement of working-class solidarity, but they've probably allowed themselves to hear what they wanted to hear. In fact, it's hard to escape the feeling that the tone is a mocking one, and as Jagger launches into "Let's drink to the two thousand million", there's more than a hint of sarcasm. Although many have taken the song at face value (Judy Collins, amongst others, who included a version on her highly successful *Judith*), but the song is as much a sneer as a salute. The Stones, and Jagger in particular, have been accused of many things in their time, but identification with working-class interests has never been one of them.

This is not to suggest that the track didn't work – indeed, it was the level of ambiguity which ensured that it did. The only real lyrical failure was *Jig-Saw Puzzle*, a weak Bob Dylan pastiche.

Lyrically, The Stones remained at their most successful when they were at their most outrageous, threatening, demonic or just plain naughty. Thus, *Parachute Woman* ("why don't you land on me?") worked well enough, but the three which most flagrantly assaulted public sensibilities were *Street Fightin' Man*, *Sympathy For The Devil* and *Stray Cat Blues*, the latter being an explicit and convincing song about under-age groupies.

As has been mentioned, The Stones were augmented on the sessions by a number of guest stars of whom only Hopkins was thanked by name. Although it had never been standard record biz practice to credit great musicians, The Stones had invariably done so. That they should have varied their practice this time is an inclination of the large amount of outside assistance they had received. The converse of this is that there is hardly any evidence throughout *Beggar's Banquet* of contributions from Brian Jones. Just as the group was

retracing its steps to its blues roots, he, ironically, was in no shape to lead the voyage of re-discovery.

The shortcomings that have been touched upon should not obscure the fact that *Beggar's Banquet* was a remarkably successful album, one of the cast-iron classics that rock has produced. It topped the charts in neither the US nor the UK, eloquent testimony to the relative failure of the band's previous work. Since most consumers have to buy records unheard, an album's immediate commercial fate depends not on its own merits but on the merits of what preceded it. This explains why *Banquet* fared less well than it should have done and, conversely, why an album like The Faces' *Ooh, La, La!* (which did make Number One) sold out of all proportion to its quality.

The due success of *Banquet* is better gauged by the facts that it sold well over a period of time; and that it aroused keen expectations in, and therefore enhanced the sales potential of, the group's succeeding albums. It was the qualities of both *Beggar's Banquet* and *Let It Bleed* that helped *Sticky Fingers* to become the group's best-selling album.

Beggar's Banquet, though, is absolutely crucial to The Stones' whole career. Firstly, and most obviously, the structure of the market was changing, with the emphasis shifting from singles to albums, and thus it was necessary for the acts which had emerged into the sixties to prove they could handle the one form as adeptly as the other – for the secret of a great album is not necessarily the sum of a dozen great singles. Occasionally, that worked as a device – *High Tide*, obviously – but in the long term the longevity of an act depended on its ability to meet the quite different challenge of album composition.

For all the excellence of *Aftermath*, The Stones had not previously risen to the challenge. They had now. *Beggar's Banquet* was majestic and authoritative, and gave The Stones' recording career a true foundation. Consider the opposite: had *Banquet* been seriously flawed, it would have been the third consecutive unsatisfactory album, and would have left the group less well equipped to meet the newly-evolving criteria of record industry success. The Beatles and The Stones had emerged at the head of one revolution – but another was now taking place. Groups like The Pink Floyd and Traffic seemed to represent the new order – and they regarded the accumulation of hit singles as a rather facile, tiresome business. The real work, the real creativity, was achieved through albums. With *Beggar's Banquet*, The Stones crossed the great divide. The album virtually ensured the longevity of the group.

The other respect in which it marked a turning-point was that Jones had faded from the picture almost completely. The situation which had been ineluctably developing and finally crystallised: The Rolling Stones had become a *de facto* two-man group, Mick Jagger and Keith Richard. There was supposed to have been another major development in The Stones' career before the end of the year. They made a film for television, the *Rolling Stones' Rock 'n' Roll Circus*.

Plans for this had been press-released in November, at which time it was announced that Traffic, Taj Mahal and Dr. John would all be appearing. It's indicative of the chaos surrounding the event that none of those artists actually participated – though Traffic were at least replaced by The Who. John Lennon and Yoko Ono, Eric Clapton and Marianne Faithfull were also involved when the show was recorded in December, and so there should nevertheless have been sufficient star quality. The group tried to simulate a circus atmosphere, and invited clowns, dwarfs, and fire-eating and knife-throwing acts. The backstage co-ordinators were reputable enough: Jimmy Miller was to produce the music; the film would be produced by Californian Sanford Liberson (who had co-produced *Performance*) and directed by Michael Lindsay-Hogg, who had done the *Jumpin' Jack Flash* promotional film. (His later work would include *Let It Be* for The Beatles.)

Filming took place at the Intertel Studios in Wembley, before an invited audience – most of whom had received invitations through applying for free tickets in *New Musical Express*.

They're the only people ever to have seen the show. The preparations had been concluded in great haste. Although only filmed at the beginning of December, it had been optimistically announced that it would be completed in time for transmission over Christmas. In fact, Jagger has never allowed it to be released.

During the day, filming had been quite successful, and the various supporting stars had gone through their routines well enough. Almost inevitably, though, the acts didn't go to schedule. By the time The Stones themselves were due to appear, audience numbers were dwindling fast, simply because many had to catch last trains and buses. The Stones' own performance thus became a farce. Whenever a new camera angle was necessary, the director was obliged to herd what was left of the audience into a new position, making sure that all the embarrassing gaps in the background were filled up.

Under these circumstances, The Stones failed to shine in their own show. Although they repeated their performance over the next two days, Jagger found neither his own nor the band's work satisfactory. Despite much excellent footage of the guest performers, the project was shelved while Jagger, who still had great faith in it as a concept, considered what could best to be done. The most imaginative idea the group had to bring the project up to scratch was for them to film their contribution in the Coliseum in Rome – scene of the world's original circuses. The Italian authorities, however, never proved amenable to the idea, so the plan was dropped. Gradually, Jagger lost interest in the project itself. The film itself remains in his possession, but he has no inclination (and certainly no need) to sanction a public showing. Presumably in fifty or a hundred years' time, a latterday Kevin Brownlow will re-discover it, and finally the *Rolling Stones' Rock 'n' Roll Circus* will be shown to the public for the first time.

Still, it was Jagger's film – his to have and to hold. The episode nevertheless invites invidious comparisons with the Beatles. After all, they did allow *Magical Mystery Tour*, their failure of a television film, to go ahead. It was embarrassingly bad, yet they refrained from locking it away and at least had the guts to make their mistakes in public. Jagger's negative policy of concealment was always the least admirable course of action.

After the filming had been completed, Mick and Keith together with Marianne and Anita flew to Rio de Janeiro, as part of a business trip. They were turned out of their hotel, because of "their untidy way of dress", but otherwise managed to avoid the headlines for once.

As it happened, the business negotiations proved abortive. During this period, The Stones were beginning to hatch more and more elaborate plans for the future. This paralleled what the Beatles were doing. Each group had reached a plateau. There were none of the traditional heights of the business left to scale, nothing more to accomplish. Accordingly, they had to boldly go where rock acts had never been before. Jagger and Richard had decided that Jones would have to be dropped, so that the band could go on an extended world tour, taking in not just South America, but also other uncharted territories such as South-East Asia. The peripatetics would conclude on stage at the Royal Albert Hall in London. There would, of course, be film and sound-crews to record their exploits, so that the enterprise would be turned into a feature film and a soundtrack album.

The projected world tour never materialised.

8

By the beginning of 1969, it was clear that The Stones had eased themselves successfully through their semi-retirement, and had additionally ensured that they could easily survive the mini-revolution that was occurring in the background as 'pop' was transformed into 'rock'. Mick and Marianne were at this stage still a close couple, having been seen in the new year in South America. Marianne had been pregnant the previous October, but had had a miscarriage a month later. Naturally, the whole business had created headlines, the initial announcement having spurred another outbreak of anti-Jagger moralising (after all, they *weren't married*), but this had obviously been dissipated – had even become something approaching sympathy – when they lost the baby.

A subtle change was taking place in the way the media treated Jagger. Up to this point, the press had relished writing, usually disparagingly, about the group. The Rolling Stones had been a permanent aunt sally. Now, Jagger was beginning to assert himself more as an individual, and to become a major public celebrity in his own right. Thus, everything that happened to him was news, and the undertones of malicious gossip began to disappear from articles about him.

During the early stages of 1969, The Stones maintained a low public profile. Jagger made a close examination of the *Rock 'n' Roll Circus* footage. It was spring before the group reassembled. Much of the next album had already been put down on tape, since the *Beggar's Banquet* sessions had yielded an abundance of material, but more tracks were still required nonetheless.

Jimmy Miller was on hand again as producer, and Glyn Johns as engineer. Jack Nitzsche flew in to London, and reported for duty to Olympic Studios. Although he was ready to help, as always, it was apparent to him that The Stones were now beginning to change in ways that were not to his liking.

Jagger and co. were in the unusual position both of being entirely their own masters, and of not having been trained or conditioned in any way to carry such personal responsibility. To all those accustomed to coping with the routine problems of life, this may not seem a grievous cross to bear. It should be evident nevertheless that such an extreme liberation can be unsettling for all but the most stable of psyches. As it happens, both Jagger and Richard were strong enough to deal with it – the former especially. Even so, they both wobbled. It was at this time that Richard began taking heroin, and encouraging his friends to use it. Jagger, less dramatically and less dangerously, took to wearing make-up quite frequently. It was such patterns

of behaviour that Nitzsche found disturbing.

Meanwhile, Jagger's screen debut had hit problems. Warner Bros., the company which had financed it, had found it to be "unintelligible". While its fate was still uncertain, however, it was announced that Jagger had signed to play the title-role in the film *Ned Kelly*, to be directed by Tony Richardson.

On the very same day that this was made public, the flat in Cheyne Walk, Chelsea, where Mick and Marianne were living, was raided by police. Jagger and Faithfull were subsequently charged with possession of cannabis; the following day, May 29, they were remanded on bail.

Brian Jones was sacked from the group on June 9. The others had deferred a decision for as long as possible, but by then the course of action was quite inescapable. The physical and mental state of Jones was not going to improve, and he was by then materially affecting the progress of the group, for they were virtually unable to tour with him as a band member.

When Jagger and Richard finally realised they had to confront him, they enlisted the support of Charlie Watts, and the three formed a deputation to give Jones his cards. A public announcement indicated that Jones had departed of his own volition. From his Hartfield home, Brian told the press that "The Stones' music is not to my taste any more. I want to play my own kind of music."

In fact, once the deed had been done, it seemed a wonderful release for both camps. Jones himself seemed happier and began to talk enthusiastically about making his own records. He reiterated his old grouse about never being able to get any of his compositions on Stones' albums – although this seemed as much a piece of self-deception at this time as it had years earlier, for there was no evidence that he ever had written songs of his own.

The others were able to announce a replacement straightaway. He was Mick Taylor, from John Mayall's Bluesbreakers. At only twenty, he seemed rather timid – certainly not the sort of person to take over one of rock music's hot seats. He had left Mayall some weeks earlier, and received a phone-call from Jagger inviting him to a recording session. It seems that he had slotted in immediately, and was quickly offered the job. Jagger allowed Richard to make the decision, since it was he who would be playing in harness with him. The former confessed to some surprise that Keith hadn't wanted to audition several hopefuls, but apparently he was satisfied with Taylor. At this point, Led Zeppelin had lately been formed. Prior to that, had Jones been ousted earlier, The Stones had been in favour of offering the

Hyde Park, 1969.

vacancy to Jimmy Page. In the event, it was Taylor who was in the right place at the right time, and once Keith had professed admiration for his playing, all was quickly settled. It was announced that his live debut with the band would take place within a month, at a free concert in Hyde Park on July 5.

This testified to their readiness to resume live engagements. Aside from that short, sharp concert in May 1968, they had not played before their own fans since their 1966 tour, and a free concert seemed an appropriate way of returning to live work in the UK. It was the kind of glorious, magnaminous gesture that would win favourable publicity. There had been a free concert in Hyde Park the previous month when Blind Faith had inaugurated their career with a triumphant performance (though the auspicious start to that band's career was highly misleading).

Before the concert took place, Brian Jones died. Just after midnight on July 3, his body was discovered at the bottom of his swimming pool at his Sussex home. Although he suffered badly from asthma, the pathologist could find no evidence that he had had an attack while taking his midnight bathe. He had, though, been taking amphetamines, and also drinking brandy. The coroner recorded a verdict of misadventure: "he drowned while under the influence of alcohol and drugs". In fact, he'd taken a sleeping-pill. With the pills and the drink, and the warmth of the pool, it is most likely that he simply fell asleep. Despite his general state of physical debilitation, the most likely explanation of his death is that it was a complete accident.

The other Stones, not unnaturally, were deeply upset. Although they had had their differences with Jones, they all seemed genuinely shocked and saddened. It was felt that the Hyde Park concert might be cancelled, but Jagger was determined that it should go ahead, and become a tribute to Jones. "Brian would have wanted it to go on," Jagger declared. "I hope people will understand that it is because of our love for him that we are still doing it."

The tragedy added an extra piquancy to what was already due to be an event of special significance. The concert, which started at 1 p.m., took place before an estimated audience of two hundred and fifty thousand on a very hot day when, elsewhere in London, Ann Jones was winning the Ladies Singles Championship at Wimbledon.

During the afternoon an interesting selection of supporting bands took the stage in turn: Third Ear Band, King Crimson, Screw, Alexis Korner's New Church, Pete Brown's Battered Ornaments, and the newly-emergent, greatly-respected Family. The Stones themselves appeared about 6 p.m., with Jagger appearing all in white, in a sort of Greek frockcoat.

He prefaced the set by reading a Shelley poem, which he said suited Brian, and releasing boxes of butterflies into the crowd. After that, it was straight into a set which effectively counterpointed songs from virtually every stage of a fascinating career. Sympathy For The

Devil was performed with the accompaniment of six African drummers.

The Stones wowed the crowd, and then found that plans for the traditional speedy exit had gone awry – after all, they were in the middle of the park. Though the concert itself must have been a relatively calming experience, with the audience reacting in an excited, but, on the whole, responsible manner, the manner of their leaving must have reminded them of the worst moments of Stones hysteria of years earlier as their getaway vehicle was besieged. The whole event had been filmed for television. It was one of the special occasions in the history of rock.

With the acclaim from press and public alike still ringing, Jagger flew off to Australia to undertake his Ned Kelly filming commitments which had almost provoked a bitter row. His producers had really wanted him out there a couple of days earlier; they would have preferred the group not to have given the free concert.

Mick was accompanied by Marianne, who was also to be given a part in the film. Ned Kelly was one of Australia's legendary outlaws, and there was special security at Sydney airport for a contemporary outlaw gang had threatened to kidnap Mick and administer a haircut. In fact, there was no problem at that stage; the problems began soon afterwards.

A matter of hours after arriving in Sydney, Marianne collapsed in her room at the Chevron Hotel and was taken unconscious to hospital. She had taken a drug overdose. She was kept in intensive care and remained in a coma for five days. Since Mick had already kept the film unit waiting, he had to start work on the production, though he at least ensured that Marianne's mother flew out to be with her daughter.

It seems that it was as a result of this kind of emotional instability that Mick's affection for Marianne began to wane. Obviously, she was unable to fulfil her own film commitments, and her part was taken by Diane Craig, an English-born actress living in Australia.

Back home, the beginning and the end of that English summer was marked by two important releases from The Stones. The first was a new single, Honky Tonk Women, another undisputed classic. It had been written by Jagger and Richard during their South American sojourn, and conveys an atmosphere of unsurpassed sleaziness. As Roy Carr points out, the song "is an object lesson in musical economy", with the taut song made more dynamic by the contributions, above all, of Richard and Watts – though Jagger, of course, demonstrated what a super-cool stylist he was in taking the song at his own pace. This showed how perfectly The Stones functioned as a group, so that it was impossible to imagine it being sung by anyone else or in any other way. (This latter point was to become interesting.)

The other side featured You Can't Always Get What You Want, a complete contrast, which had been conceived almost as a choral work, as Jagger sung it not only with three girl vocalists – Madeleine Bell, Doris Troy and Nanette Newman – but also the London Bach Choir.

When summer was ending, their second hits album, *Through The Past, Darkly*, came on the market. As on the previous occasion with *High Tide*, the group showed great judgement in putting the compilation together. They made it as a kind of tribute to Jones, gave it an arresting title, and put it out in an octagonal sleeve. The tracks covered the hit singles released since the last compilation (six tracks, since two singles were double A-sides), together with those two stand-out tracks from *Satanic Majesties*, a *Beggar's Banquet* track, one earlier album track, *You Better Move On*, previously only available on EP, and *Sittin' On The Fence*, not previously available in the UK at all. Most importantly the running order was carefully arranged so that it was an effective album in its own right.

Other events in the annals of The Stones that summer took place without their direct participation: a son, Marlon, was born to Keith Richard and Anita Pallenberg on August 10; and the Edinburgh Film Festival premiered both Godard's *One Plus One* and the Hyde Park film. There was other film news: Richard took a cameo part in *Michael Kohlass*, starring Anita and David Warner and Warner Bros., despite having found *Performance* unintelligible, at least revised their instinctive decision simply to abandon it.

Jagger spent the summer – or, rather, the winter – filming *Ned Kelly* in Australia. After enjoying a brief holiday in Indonesia he spent just twenty-four hours in London before flying, with the others, to the States for the group's first US tour for over three years.

Once Mick Taylor had been drafted into the line-up, there was no impediment to the resumption of live performances, and so dates in various countries had been arranged at the earliest opportunity. News that The Stones would shortly be back in business travelled quickly, and a completely false rumour, that they would be playing in Berlin had actually prompted a riot there – shades of happenings three years earlier.

Genuine tickets on sale in the US had been snapped up within hours. The tour was not an extensive one but it did take in fourteen cities. By now, audiences were older and the crowd reactions, though still frenzied, were less hysterical. The opening gig at the Inglewood Forum in Los Angeles was notable largely for the lack of organisation. The Stones were due to play two concerts, at 7 and 11 p.m. In the event, they didn't take the stage for the *first* one until eleven. The fault wasn't theirs but due to maladministration at the venue, where an ice hockey match had been playing during the afternoon. Hardly surprisingly, the ice had interfered with the deployment of the Stones' sound system but despite everything the shows did go on -- however belatedly. The second concert finished at 5.15 a.m. but the final ovation was a tumultuous one nevertheless.

In Palm Springs, the group encountered opposition from the ultra-right-wing John Birch Society who claimed, with little originality and less accuracy, that the group was corrupting the moral character of youth. The show went ahead as planned. Later in the itinerary, concerts at Madison Square Garden on November 28 & 29 were recorded for a future live album.

The tour closed with a free concert. It was a relatively impromptu offering from the group stimulated partly at least by a wish to defuse the undercurrent of niggling criticism during the tour due to the high price of tickets. In offering a free concert, though, The Stones doubtless also had in mind the success of their own Hyde Park summer show. A month later, in the US, there had been the phenomenal triumph of the Woodstock open-air festival. The Stones wished to hold a celebratory event of their own.

The concert took place at Altamont, on a drag-racing track in the hills just outside Tracy, California. It was not a triumph. Instead it is remembered as the occasion which illuminated the dark underside of the Woodstock generation. The Stones asked a local chapter of the Hell's Angels to act as stewards (as indeed they had at the Hyde Park concert; these particular Angels had been recommended by Jerry Garcia of the Grateful Dead), as by now they recognised the need to try to maintain some sort of order at the front of the audience. With a crowd of up to five hundred thousand some sort of policing was necessary.

As it turned out, the most charitable view of the Angels' conduct is that they acted over-zealously. Few people, however, would have been inclined to be charitable. To them, it seemed that the Angels had merely behaved with characteristic brutality, in either repressing the more excitable elements in the crowd or actually provoking violence for its own sake. While Jagger was singing on stage, the Angels stabbed to death one member of the audience – an incident that is recorded in all its horror in the David and Albert Mayles' film of the event, *Gimme Shelter*.

The main problem was the lack of control which The Stones themselves had been able to exercise. In the first place, the scheme seemed jinxed because the site had been moved several times. Richard had, with some foresight, wanted the whole thing called off. Secondly, the Angels had simply taken control themselves. During Jefferson Airplane's afternoon set Marty Balin had been injured in a disturbance between fans and angels. The mood was certainly turning ugly.

Things deteriorated rapidly, and the murder directly in front of the stage actually occurred as Jagger was singing *Sympathy For The Devil*. As can be seen from the film, The Stones didn't know how to deal with it. Richard at least reacted angrily and assertively. Jagger seemed scared and unsure of how to react. Certainly, the set should have been stopped. With murder taking place in front of your eyes, this was no time to apply the old adage that "the show must go on". Yet, that is exactly what happened. Most of the audience were unaware of the tragic turn of events until the following

day.

Jagger had not reacted positively or responsibly, and Altamont became a watchword to haunt The Stones. Once too often, it seemed, Jagger had flirted with the dark forces: *Satanic Majesties, Jumpin' Jack Flash, Sympathy For The Devil*. The group had also espoused the notions of androgyny and violence which, taken together and with the material, almost did point to an alliance with the underworld. Altamont had forged the link. It was almost as though Jagger was in league with the Devil – could perhaps be Lucifer himself, performing on stage, goading and inciting his acolytes – Hell's Angels – and presiding over chaos and destruction. Jagger had previously been visualised as the minister for sex and drugs. Then, there followed the outlaw stage. Now, there were those who considered that he represented Lucifer. The whole notion was scary and frightening.

Were The Stones the real Satanic Majesties after all? Though the press – in the US especially – had a field day in making such innuendos, a calmer analysis utterly rejected such base theories. Even so, the most sympathetic observer would have had to admit that perhaps Jagger had planted too many clues for his own good, and that The Stones had been dabbling in areas they didn't understand, and energising forces they couldn't control like the sorcerer's apprentice. Altamont seemed to be nemesis.

Their whole history had shown their concern with adopting antithetical poses, whether it was anti-culture, anti-society, anti-establishment or anti-Christ. To maintain their rebellious momentum, they kept needing to embrace more and more extreme concepts. It had been a literally irresponsible attitude, and suddenly they were faced with the problem of needing to deal with its consequences. For the first time, they were burdened with a sense of responsibility.

This marks the real turning-point in the history both of the Stones and of Jagger himself, the group's true guiding-spirit. While edging ever closer to the privileges which the rich and powerful enjoy, Jagger had always maintained his anti-establishment stance. His whole career was based on this lie, this ability to dissemble, to adopt practised and plausible public poses. After Altamont, Jagger could no longer behave in a Janus fashion.

The most immediately apparent effect, of course, was that Jagger immediately dropped the saturnine imagery that had been a feature both of The Stones' compositions and of their mystique as a group, and it has never reappeared.

Some critics have inferred that the way The Stones handled Altamont showed their sure instinct for survival as a group. Obviously, they did survive it, largely through a refusal to openly concede that they were in any way responsible for what had happened. But they were, however, and the concert casts them in a different light. Their lack of moral fibre is made painfully apparent. In refusing to come to terms with

events either at the time or later, the situation shows how cowardly they could be. After all, once the concert had finished, they couldn't get out of America fast enough. Hoping to leave their feelings of guilt behind them, no doubt.

As it happened, Jagger did have reason to behave in a frightened manner. Members of The Stones' audience weren't the only ones dismayed by his behaviour. The Hell's Angels considered that he had betrayed them, and accordingly put out a contract on his life. They twice tried to assassinate him. This information only came to light in March 1983 when a former Angel's chapter leader testified to a Senate judiciary committee hearing on the links between motorcycle gangs and organised crime. Moreover, the threats to Jagger were still present. The former gang member inferred that, having tried twice and failed, the Angels were unlikely to be thwarted a third time.

In every respect, therefore, Altamont was the price the Stones paid for years of self-indulgent, irresponsible rebellion. The murder at the concert provided a chilling finale to *Gimme Shelter*, just as the concert itself put a full-stop to rock's age of innocence. Nothing was really the same after Altamont.

Back in Britain, The Stones played dates in London at the Saville Theatre in Shaftesbury Avenue (the venue that had been purchased by Brian Epstein some years earlier) and, seven days later, at the Lyceum just off the Strand. Tickets for both concerts sold out almost immediately. The group had wanted to perform at the Royal Albert Hall, though the management there declined to accept a booking for them, for fear of fans causing damage to that hallowed auditorium. In fact, both concerts passed off without undue incident.

Between the two gigs, Mick's latest drug bust, postponed since May, finally came to court. He was charged with Marianne. She was acquitted, but he was fined two hundred pounds, plus costs, for being in possession of cannabis. The most important effect of this conviction was that the US Immigration Authorities imposed an 18-month delay on issuing Jagger with an American visa.

Although he had ensured that he had attended the trial with Marianne, it transpired at this time that the two had parted company a month earlier: the second major affair of Jagger's life had reached its natural end.

Let It Bleed was released in December. This was a worthy companion-piece to *Beggar's Banquet* (after all, tracks from both albums had been recorded at the same sessions) and evinced the same strengths as its predecessor, particularly the instrumental clarity and the blues-based nature of the material. *Gimme Shelter* this time served as the strong opening track, and *Love In Vain* was the blues number following it which provided a stylistic contrast.

The most controversial track was *Midnight Rambler*, a song which drew its atmosphere of danger and malevolence from the exploits of the infamous mass-murderer, the Boston Strangler. Certainly, Jagger

could whip up a charge of real menace when delivering it on stage. It was actually the conjunction of the release of this track with the awful tragedy of Altamont which convinced so many people that The Stones were actually involved with satanic forces.

The country-styled *You Got The Silver* was sung by Keith Richard – the first Stones track on which Jagger didn't appear at all. It was chosen by Antonioni for the soundtrack of *Zabriskie Point*.

Interestingly, both sides of the previous single were included – though in different forms. *You Can't Always Get What You Want* was a lengthier, seven-minute treatment. Most surprisingly, though, *Honky Tonk Women* appeared as a country song, with a prominent fiddle part contributed by Byron Berline, one of the

musicians who had been introduced to The Stones as a result of Keith's developing friendship with Gram Parsons, then a member of the Flying Burrito Brothers (who had also appeared at Altamont). The number was the last to have been recorded, and had only been polished off at Elektra's studios in Hollywood in November.

It was an album which showed The Stones expanding their range but from the basis of the blues-based rock which they had mastered. One postscript about the album's release concerns the London Bach Choir, duly and properly credited for their part in *You Can't Always Get What You Want*. They did not welcome the album at all: it featured tracks like *Live With Me*, which had distasteful lyrics; *Midnight Rambler* was

utterly repugnant, and both the cover and the title were deliberately unpleasant. The London Bach Choir could not erase their contribution from the record – but they insisted on having their name erased from the credits. Decca duly obliged with a large black patch.

At the beginning of 1970, *Let It Bleed* was riding high in the charts the world over, but The Stones themselves were psychologically depressed by Altamont and its aftermath, and so they actually managed what they'd been trying to achieve for some time – and spent a year lying low. In fact, they were casting their eyes over property in the South of France. Richard was the only one who had good reason to be doing this, since he was worried that Anita would not be allowed to remain in the UK (unless, of course, he married her). The others were merely thinking of becoming tax exiles.

As usual, they made sure of keeping on top of their

James Fox, Cecil Beaton and Mick Jagger in a scene from *Performance*.

recording schedule, recording new material throughout the early summer both in London and at Stargroves, Jagger's country home in Berkshire, where they used their mobile recording truck.

The album which was released however, and which almost completed the Decca contract, was *Get Yer Ya-Yas Out*, the live album recorded at Madison Square Garden the previous winter. Jagger had originally wanted this to be a double, with the second album featuring one side of music from each of the other acts on the tour, B. B. King and Ike & Tina Turner. It's a pity this idea never came to fruition, as it was a particularly intriguing one and, who knows, might even have set a welcome precedent. It was said that contractual difficulties prevented the release of the double, but in truth Decca weren't interested in pursuing the idea. By then they knew that The Stones wouldn't be staying with them, so there was no point in trying to accomodate them.

All the material came from the recent resurgent past, though a couple of Chuck Berry numbers had been included for old time's sake. It was a powerful album, which captured the excitement of the original concert, and was buoyed particularly by the way Jagger improvised some of the material to develop a dialogue with the audience; *Midnight Rambler* and *Sympathy For The Devil* were the tracks concerned. The renditions, of course, had predated Altamont.

To fulfil their Decca contract, The Stones still needed to provide Decca with one extra, new song. So they sent the tape of *Cocksucker Blues*. This was later re-titled *Schoolboy Blues* for public performance (in *The Trials Of Oz*) and is quite an effective song. Decca, naturally, blushed as deeply as Jagger had intended and accepted that The Stones were no longer their artists.

The group had already parted company with Allan Klein, on the day before the technical expiry of the Decca contract. Lawyers acting for the group advised Klein that neither he nor his companies were to be involved in any way in negotiating a new recording contract. Jagger – so good at courting publicity, so good at concealing what could be concealed – never revealed the precise reasons for their dissatisfaction with Klein, but it seems likely that he had siphoned off lots of their earnings for his own purposes and indeed, just before the Beatles had got involved with him, the London *Sunday Times* had run a front-page report detailing irregularities in Klein's handling of the Stones' finances. The paper warned the Beatles to stay clear. It was good advice which the Beatles (or three of them) ignored. Once The Stones had severed their association with him in a rancorous fashion, the Beatles were left with a great deal of egg on their faces.

Both of Jagger's films opened during the summer of 1970 – *Ned Kelly* was premiered in Australia in July and *Performance* opened in New York in August. *Ned Kelly* was not an inspired film and its director, Tony Richardson, was fast losing the cachet he had acquired earlier in the sixties. *Performance* was altogether more

electrifying, as Roeg had tried to draw a link between the lives of criminals and those of rock stars; Jagger as outlaw, again. The themes were complex, so that it was not surprising that Warner Bros executives had found the film hard to comprehend. Equally, its complexities have sent audiences returning to it again and again, and since its premier hardly a week has passed when the film hasn't been showing somewhere. Jagger's own performance was measured and confident. *Ned Kelly* was different. Jagger, in a beard and Australian accent, was not at all convincing, and the film was mediocre. It is still shown occasionally today, but that is simple curiosity interest because it is Jagger in the title-role.

Taken together, the films did not encourage Jagger to turn from rock 'n' roll to the cinema. Perhaps if *Ned Kelly* had been delayed, instead of *Performance*, he might have received the positive reaction from the latter which would have encouraged him to pursue that direction further. As it was though, *Performance*, which vindicated him, arrived only after he had received very discouraging notices for *Ned Kelly*.

On the whole, he is simply too prestigious a name as a rock performer, and the cinema could never have been more than an occasional side-line. What probably deterred him still further from films was that he was almost killed during work on *Ned Kelly*, when an ancient pistol blew up as he was holding it.

The Stones went on the road again in the autumn with an extensive continental tour. For the first time, they were properly augmented, with Nicky Hopkins on piano and two Americans, Bobby Keyes (saxophone) and Jim Price (trumpet). The latter two had attached themselves to The Stones camp in the spring, via a circuitous route. They had played on the sensationally exciting Delaney & Bonnie tour. Eric Clapton, who'd sponsored and played with them, had then taken three members of D&B's band to form Derek & the Dominoes, and had also sent plane tickets to Keyes and Price. They returned to the UK, but never sealed an agreement with Clapton. Instead, they played on George Harrison's *All Things Must Pass* and then moved on to Olympic Studios where The Stones were recording. Keyes and Price joined The Stones entourage, and stayed for several years.

At the end of October, Marianne Faithfull was divorced by her husband, John Dunbar, who cited Jagger's adultery as grounds for his petition. Of course, Mick and Marianne had long since split up. It was just ironic that as this was going through the courts, so a new liaison of Jagger's was coming to the attention of the press. He was seen at Heathrow airport with Bianca Perez Moreno de Macias. "We're just good friends", Jagger told reporters, helpfully.

The year closed with the opening in New York of *Gimme Shelter*, a film that all too vividly documented the rousing excitement of The Stones' performance at the concert, and the equally frenzied response of the audience.

9

On March 4, 1971 The Rolling Stones announced they would be going into tax exile. In some respects, this seemed the ultimate snub to their fans. Having made their name by striking a number of quasi-revolutionary poses, they were now seeking the sanctuary of the chronically rich and not even having the decency to pay their taxes and support the social and economic system which had enabled them to flourish.

Of course, it had been obvious for some time that sooner or later some rock stars would seek to shield their massive incomes from the demands made upon them by a welfare state, but it had not previously happened. This was one area in which The Stones really did set a precedent. It happened, furthermore, at the moment when The Stones were just beginning to earn sizeable monies – i.e. now that they had negotiated an exceptionally favourable recording contract.

On the other hand, there were some reasons which Jagger and co. had for quitting the country which were not dishonourable. Basically, they were all becoming rather paranoid; there had been few periods in recent years when one or other of them was not being persecuted. Paradoxically, Britain had become the place where they felt least at home.

Jagger would have felt his decision to move abroad vindicated almost immediately, for later in March he was once again the victim of a raid by the police drugs squad. As it happened, charges were not pressed on that occasion, perhaps because it was too transparently a put-up job. (Photographers had arrived outside the flat even before the police.) It served, though, as a convenient reminder for Jagger that he and the others – and in particular Keith and himself – were vulnerable to continual police harrassment while they remained resident in the country.

There was a brief farewell tour, lasting from March 4-14, which naturally aroused great interest; at several venues, thousands queued all day for tickets. At the conclusion of the tour, they recorded two shows at the Marquee for television transmission during their absence. In fact, none of the companies to whom the film was screened (the BBC, Thames, London Weekend) elected to purchase it, and the shows have never been seen in the UK (only on the continent); perhaps it was just as well that Jagger never bothered to finish the *Rock 'n' Roll Circus*.

Details of the group's new recording contract were announced on April 7. They had signed with Kinney (WEA) and arranged a deal for their own Rolling Stones Records to be distributed through Atlantic. This suited them perfectly. (So much so that they had plumped for Atlantic despite higher offers from two other

companies). Atlantic was a prestigious name to be associated with and had masterminded the careers of a number of celebrated acts who, like Ray Charles and the Coasters, had represented particular peaks of achievement in the history of black popular music. Further, The Stones actually had their own company and label within Atlantic, so they would (or so they imagined) be able to avoid the kind of interminable iconoclastic-artist/cautious-publisher rows that had pockmarked their relationship with Decca.

They appointed Marshall Chess to head the new operation. This, too, seemed auspicious. He was the son of the founder of Chess Records, the company which had so successfully marketed the very music which had brought the group together in the first place. In fact, the promise of this particular appointment was never realised. Rolling Stones Records – with a slavering tongue as its logo existed just as the label on which The Stones' own recordings appeared. It never functioned as a proper company with the aim of acquiring and promoting new talent. Further, such company business as there was tended to be channelled directly through Jagger. Marshall Chess discovered that he had been given responsibility but no power. He resigned in 1976.

The announcement of the deal had been made in New York – appropriately, since that was where Atlantic was based. It could not have been made from London. By then, at the start of the tax year, the group were officially domiciled in France. During April, May and June they tackled work on a new double-album, recording it on their own mobile which was now parked outside Richard's home of Nellcote, Villefranche-sur-Mer, situated between Nice and Monte Carlo. As its name indicates, it was on the coast.

While recording was in progress Bianca was pregnant, so Mick kept absenting himself from the sessions to be with her in Paris. This was not a insignificant development in The Stones' career, for Richard increasingly found himself in solitary charge of proceedings, so that he began to think of The Stones as his band. His major creative influence became quite apparent when *Exile On Main Street* was released.

Its predecessor, *Sticky Fingers*, was released in April 1971, together with a single that included three tracks – *Brown Sugar*, *Bitch* and *Let It Rock*, only the latter of which was not also available on the album.

Sticky Fingers became the group's best-selling album. As has been pointed out, it benefitted from the positive momentum built up by the two previous albums, as well as from the fact that it was the first album under a new contract and therefore the distributors were especially attentive to matters of publicity and promotion. It is remarkable how often even established artists will achieve significantly greater success than usual with the first fruits of a new contract.

Lyrically, the album was notable for avoiding the kind of statements of social or political outrage that had invited trouble in the past. This was a chastened, post-Altamont Jagger; he was keeping a clean nose this time. In fact, *Sticky Fingers* marked a turning-point. From this album on, with increasingly rare exceptions, Jagger has written songs with the lyrical parameters – sex, drugs, cars – of mainstream rock 'n' roll itself. They have been no more or less adventurous than that.

On *Sticky Fingers* itself, by way of compensation – or perhaps revenge – for presiding over this emasculation of the band's work, Jagger crammed the album full of overt and covert drug references, and also put it out in a deliberately provocative cover (though it seems tame enough today). It had been designed by Andy Warhol and caused a number of production problems. It depicted, simply, a male crotch, fully clothed, but with a real zip in the middle, teasingly waiting to be unzipped. A sexually stimulating motif perhaps but on a more mundane level, the device is remembered largely for the fact that it destroyed the sleeve of any record filed next to it.

The music was of two types. There was much that was typical Stones' stuff – raw and rhythmic, loud and aggressive – particularly the opening tracks on each side *Brown Sugar*, a single which admirably sustained the traditions of *Jumpin' Jack Flash* and *Honky Tonk Women*, and *Bitch* which benefited from the addition of the brass section. Otherwise, *Can't You Hear Me Knocking* was the most urgent, vibrant track, noted for some pulsating interplay between the saxophone and the guitars of Taylor and Richard.

On the other hand, there was an unusual number of slower tracks. Indeed, those who considered that the group purveyed only the solid diet of high energy rock 'n' roll would have been amazed to note how many tracks opened with Richard playing acoustic guitar. There were two country songs – *Wild Horses* (written about Anita Pallenberg, at the time that Mick and Marianne were breaking up), which had been recorded first by the Flying Burrito Brothers, and *Dead Flowers*, perhaps the best in that vein that The Stones have ever delivered; it was on that song that Jagger first adopted his famous Nashville drawl, which readily identifies The Stones' material of a country flavour.

The closing *Moonlight Mile* was a more significant departure. The most adventurous track, it was a stately ballad, which featured string arrangements by Paul Buckmaster; *I Got The Blues* was another affectionate return to the Stax sounds of the '60s; and then there was *Sister Morphine*, one of the more controversial tracks (the Spanish distributors, for example, replaced it by *Let It Rock*). A version of this had been released two years earlier by Marianne Faithfull – when she had claimed a co-composition credit. The Stones' own version had also been recorded two years earlier –

when both Ry Cooder and Jack Nitzsche were present – and Faithful is not credited with having helped write the song.

Altogether it was an excellent album – thoroughly deserving of becoming, in commercial terms at least, the group's premier work.

Meanwhile, Decca, sensing that their loss was indeed someone else's gain, inaugurated a policy of issuing cheapskate compilations of Stones' numbers to which they owned the rights. Since there was a considerable amount of Stones' material which, for one reason or another, was not on catalogue, the task of making this work more widely available could have been approached in a sensible and worthwhile fashion. The company however, took the most exploitative course available – allowing previously hard-to-get material out in a trickle, and filling out the albums with songs that most loyal Stones' fans would have acquired more than once already.

It was not a longsighted or prudent policy. It did not deserve to succeed, and it didn't. The Stones took out advertisements in the British music press to express their disapproval of the first product of this policy, *Stone Age*. (The group would no doubt have been further infuriated by the cover of the album which illustrated precisely the kind of graffiti art which they had wanted to use for *Beggar's Banquet*, and to which Decca had so stubbornly objected). In the entire history of the record industry, Decca has much of which it can be justly proud. Its shabby and hypocritical treatment of The Stones' catalogue, however, forms one of the company's more murky chapters.

On May 12, Mick and Bianca married in St. Tropez Town Hall, in front of rather too many photographers for comfort. The wedding perfectly illuminated the contradictions in the Jagger mystique. After all, much of the occasion smacked of high society etiquette: everything proceeded with impeccable decorum, Bianca – pregnant albeit – dressed all in white and Jagger himself wore a three-piece suit. There were actually two ceremonies – a civil one, followed by a Roman Catholic one (in preparation for which Jagger had been taking special instruction). The magazine *Rolling Stone* entered into the spirit of the occasion by publishing a formal guest-list.

The guest themselves – many of whom had arrived direct from Gatwick airport on a specially-chartered plane – made an interesting selection. There were the anticipated number of rockbiz celebrities – Paul McCartney and Ringo Starr and their wives, Stephen Stills, Doris Troy and Ronnie Lane; there were those previously associated with The Stones' social circle – Christopher Gibbs and Donald Cammell; there were names from the *beau monde* of swinging London – Ossie Clark and Lord (Patrick) Lichfield; and those who more familiarly moved in Bianca's social circle in Paris – Roger Vadim and Natalie Delon.

Jagger did his best to retain his rock 'n' roll credentials by dispensing with a tie, and it should also be

Jerry Hall shows off her ranch – a present from Mick.

mentioned that the music was provided by Stills, Troy, Bobby Keyes, Nicky Hopkins and others, and that it pounded away until four in the morning. The rock 'n' roll spirit that pervaded the post-nuptial celebrations contrasted oddly with that which Bianca had requested should be played in church: selections from the soundtrack of *Love Story*.

The Jaggers' daughter, Jade, their only child, was born on October 21.

The marriage had two important effects on Jagger. The first was that, as the *Exile On Main Street* sessions had already revealed, he deferred to Bianca far more than the rest of the group would have wished, and frequently interrupted or cut short sessions in order to be with her. Richard's relationship with Anita had never affected the group, since from her time with Brian Jones she had been easily absorbed into its slipstream. Bianca, by contrast, was never a rock 'n' roll wife and always stood apart from the group. There was no possible way in which Jagger could reconcile her demands and those of The Rolling Stones: it had to be one or the other.

Secondly, Bianca was already accustomed to indulging herself in the social whirl and comporting with the jet-sets of at least two continents. These were just the circles in which Jagger himself wanted to move. Even though he sometimes pretended otherwise, he liked to consider himself at ease with the rich and fashionable. Bianca opened up many doors for him, and the two became regular habitue's of *le plus chic* party and club circuits. A Mick and Bianca story became the standby of every gossip columnist.

Such extensions of Jagger's social calendar were reinforced by the fact that since the launch of Rolling Stones Records he'd become friendly with Atlantic president Ahmet Ertegun. With him he made the social rounds in New York. In such ways, Jagger lost touch with his roots. It wasn't only Keith Richard who was contemptuous of such changes in Jagger's lifestyle.

The marriage progressed smoothly in its early years. Although the gossip columnists kept their pencils poised, they were usually recording their activities together rather than apart. There was a spate of Mick-and-Bianca headlines towards the end of 1972, after an earthquake in Nicaragua, Bianca's home country, had resulted in a serious loss of life. The Jaggers left London and flew to Kingston, Jamaica, where they chartered an aircraft to the country's capital, Managua, in order to ensure that Bianca's mother was safe. They arrived in the country on December 31, bearing two thousand typhoid injections and other vital medical supplies, to find Mrs. Macias unharmed.

On January 10, 1973 Jagger announced that The Stones would be giving a benefit concert at the Los Angeles Forum for the victims of the earthquake. The concert, which took place eight days later, was the only important one that the group has ever given for charity. It raised more than two hundred thousand pounds and by May 9 Mick and Bianca were able to fly to Washington and donate to the Senate a contribution of three hundred and fifty thousand pounds towards the Pan-American Development Fund.

This was one of the inadvertent ways in which the couple maintained their high public profile. In other respects, they courted publicity. It was hardly surprising that they were frequently nominated as best-dressed man & woman about town (or similar), especially since Bianca had a sharp and sophisticated sartorial sense.

Gradually, however, the situation changed. Mick and Bianca seemed to be enjoying the ultimate modern marriage, as they were seen individually at more and more social engagements. There was not, initially, any suggestion that the marriage itself was at risk. It was Mick's relationship with Jerry Hall, the American model and former girlfriend of Bryan Ferry, that finally undermined the partnership in 1977.

A divorce petition was served in May 1978 and was the signal for a protracted bout of legal wrangling to begin. The prime cause of this was Bianca's insistence that divorce proceedings should be heard in California. The reason for this was that the state courts tended to be unusually sympathetic to the female party in divorce hearings. Jagger naturally contested this, and the argument continued for some months, during which some highly-paid legal brains tried to determine in which country Mr. Jagger was actually resident. Finally, the case was heard in London, much to Mick's satisfaction, and the long-running divorce proceedings were concluded on November 2, 1979. Bianca was granted a decree nisi on the grounds of Mick's adultery with Jerry Hall. Bianca obtained custody of Jade, with the proviso that Mick was allowed reasonable access to her.

The question of maintenance took another year to settle after that, and on November 5, 1980 Bianca came away with a lump sum somewhere in the region of five hundred thousand pounds. During the divorce wranglings, Mick and Bianca had remained on reasonably good terms. However, once the question of alimony arose, relations became increasingly embittered, and the vestiges of their relationship disintegrated. One result was that Bianca virtually ceded custody of Jade to Jagger and she now lives in his New York apartment, overlooking Central Park, and goes to school in the city.

Early in 1972 The Stones made what retrospectively transpired to be a half-hearted attempt to use their own label purposefully, to make available works which would not otherwise have seen the light of day. The first album was *Jamming With Edward*, credited jointly to Bill Wyman, Charlie Watts, Jagger, Nicky Hopkins and Ry Cooder. During early sessions for *Let It Bleed* relations between the two guitarists, Cooder and Richard, deteriorated to the point where Richard walked out. The album thus consists of material recorded in his absence, as the others simply jammed together and allowed the tapes to run.

Nevertheless there seemed little aesthetic validity for making material of such a sloppy character available.

Although it was competitively priced in the mid-price range, it seemed a rip-off nevertheless. There was more point to the album issued alongside it: recordings of the pipes and drums of Joujouka made by Brian Jones during his Moroccan visit of 1966. Apart from these recordings, however, no items of Stones' apocrypha have ever emerged.

The real new Stones product arrived in late spring, with a single, *Tumbling Dice* paving the way for the album, *Exile On Main Street*.

In the UK, the album raced straightaway to Number One, though it stayed there just one solitary week and altogether met with only short-lived success and disappointing sales. Yet this must be reconciled with the claims now advanced by some critics that this is one of the group's most fully-realised works.

Much of the music was undoubtedly excellent – first-class rasping rock, delivered with The Stones' inimitable panache. Right from the opening track, *Rocks Off*, the fiery level was never doused. The whole double-album packed a powerful punch. As was typical of The Stones' music of the period, the album included some country-styled material; *Sweet Virginia*, an on-the-road song, led the way. The subject-matter, in line with the new policy, adhered strictly, and

unimaginatively, to those matters within the ambit of rock 'n' roll as it was most narrowly-defined – sex, drugs, cars and the rock 'n' roll lifestyle itself. One exception, perhaps, was *Sweet Black Angel*, dedicated to the black power activist, Angela Davis.

So why was the public response so lukewarm? The first reason, clearly, is that it was a double-album, and therefore that much more difficult to assimilate. This factor was also important as far as the original reviews were concerned; the immediate critical reception was a mixed one – it was only with the benefit of hindsight (or hind-hearing) that critics became more whole-heartedly enthusiastic. By then, of course, the unfavourable reception had played a not inconsiderable part in depressing sales of the record.

Another problem was that there was no obvious stand-out track. *Tumbling Dice* had considerable charm, though it was a comparatively weak single nevertheless. The Stones' three previous classic albums had all contained tracks which impressed themselves individually upon the listener – *Street Fightin' Man*, *Gimme Shelter* and *Brown Sugar* for example – which helped to make the album as a whole more approachable. In some ways, therefore, *Exile On Main Street* actually suffered from the uniformly high standard.

The final difficulty, which has never been commented upon, is that the cover was particularly unappealing. Indeed, for a double album, the whole package was unattractive. This certainly helps to explain why the album was unloved, and is one that provides one of the very few examples in the rock industry of the design of the sleeve actually having a baleful influence on the record inside it, by discouraging consumer interest.

The album therefore remains a curiosity. It was something which seemed to leave the group's career becalmed at the time, but which has only increased in prestige in the years since.

During June and July 1972 The Stones undertook a major North American tour, one of that has become enshrined in the mythology of the group – largely because it was the first of the post-sixties tours, metaphorically as well as literally. The hysteria of the earlier years was now forgotten, as were the relatively straightened circumstances in which the group had toured. Now, the whole thing turned into a huge celebration, with vast audiences flocking to see the group which had survived to become a rock music monument, an institution, the premier band extant now that The Beatles had departed the scene. Audiences were older, and more respectful. They screamed less, but revered more. They went because The Stones were The Stones, and a Stones concert was an occasion. The horrors of Altamont had been wiped clean from the memory bank.

For The Stones themselves, it was also a whole new experience. With their new record contract and new American bosses, the whole trip turned into a much more lavish affair, with an unusually large retinue all enjoying themselves on the grand scale. After all, as The Stones played larger venues, so they needed a larger staff to set them up, so the whole business became more time-consuming – but when tours did happen, they happened in style.

The tour itself is chronicled in detail in Robert Greenfield's book, *Stones Touring Party* and was famous, amongst other things, for the fact that Jagger invited along Truman Capote and Princess Lee Radziwill for a few days. By that time, The Stones oozed celebrity – something which Richard may have regretted, but which Jagger relished.

The supporting star on the tour was Stevie Wonder, and within a year he had established himself as a major name in the rock firmament. This was thus a minor tradition that was inaugurated in 1972 – the instant elevation of the support act. Henceforward, support spots on Stones' tours were especially highly-prized. Jagger always picked the acts personally though, so competition was pointless. In general, he chose black performers who fitted in with the Atlantic heritage, and whose act complemented The Stones' own.

The major tradition established by the 1972 tour was simply that of the rock 'n' roll tour as spectacle, as carnival, as extravaganza, as triumphal procession. The tour itself became an event – far more than had ever been the case in the sixties, when fans tended to be concerned only with dates in their own home town, and when the pressures of touring on the major acts were such that one tour segued into another.

In the seventies, as tours became ever more complex administratively, they were undertaken sparingly, so that each acquired a distinct character. Tours were given *names*, they were promoted with posters and T-shirts. Tours were chronicled in exhaustive detail as Greenfield did for the 1972 jamboree. This was an entirely new style, and it was The Stones who had developed it.

The 1972 US dates set the pattern for The Stones' work throughout the decade. They toured as infrequently as monarchy – appropriately, since their tours did become regal processions. Compared with the sixties events moved slowly, and the group members became accustomed to living their own lives, and assembling only for recording sessions, rehearsals, and touring itself. This enabled Jagger, in company with Bianca, to cultivate the society image which Keith Richard so deprecated.

Partly as a result, perhaps, of the fact that he became more a pillar of the establishment than a scourge of it, Jagger seemed that much less of a threat, and suffered remarkably little harrassment from the forces of authority during the seventies. The drugs busts continued without relief, but with one exception they all entrapped Richard. (The solitary other Stone to fall foul of international drug laws was Ron Wood.)

The most publicised legal problem suffered by Jagger – apart from the divorce imbroglio – was a civil action brought by the UK singer Marsha Hunt, who claimed paternity damages from Mick on behalf of her daughter, Karis. The court action took several years to be settled. Jagger was finally forced to pay damages, though the case was never conclusively proved, and Marsha Hunt's own career had ground to a halt in the meantime.

After the disappointment of the critical and public reaction to *Exile On Main Street*, the group's recording career faltered. *Goat's Head Soup* was released in August 1973, preceded by a single, *Angie*. This was an unprecedented kind of song for the group: it used strings, and lyrically it showed Mick being chivalrous, rather than discourteous to, and contemptuous of, women. It was also an unprecedented selection for a group 45 release, since it was a ballad. No-one could dispute its staggering success in restoring the band to the top echelons of singles charts throughout the world. Richard often alluded to the fact that its very success had been double-edged, for it had overshadowed the rest of the album: exactly the opposite kind of problem to that which befell *Exile On Main Street*.

Goat's Head Soup had been recorded at Dynamic Sound Studios in Kingston, Jamaica, and did feature the stylistic range that had been missing from *Exile* (that much, indeed, had been evident from *Angie* and its B side, *Silver Train*, a fast blues number with wailing harmonica; this song, also on the album, had been originally written for Johnny Winter). One of the outstanding tracks was *Star, Star*, which was straight out of the Chuck Berry mould, with superb guitar from Richard and brilliant vocals from Jagger, lasciviously

delivering one of the great songs about groupies. It was properly called *Starfucker*, a title which Jagger had blithely assumed would be perfectly acceptable to everyone. After all, it was their record company, wasn't it? However, Atlantic, as distributors, declined to have anything to do with it. Jagger therefore, avoided another *Beggar's Banquet* type dispute by altering the title.

The other tracks were all interesting. The choice of recording location had clearly been made with a view to introducing a fresh rhythmic element to The Stones' recordings, and this was most evident in tracks like *Doo Doo Doo Doo Doo (Heartbreaker)*, which also benefited from a Jim Price horn arrangement. *Winter* was an exceptional ballad. Altogether, it was a fine album. The major problem was that fans were beginning to feel the group was declining as a recording force. The Stones had stopped being a singles band, and some of their audience had not yet tumbled to the fact that it was necessary to look elsewhere for their recording high-spots. They were not investigating the albums properly.

There were two further difficulties: firstly, there was still a tendency to expect too much of the group; and secondly there was no longer material calculated to shock, because Jagger had deliberately eschewed that after Altamont. Yet that kind of controversial song had always been useful in stimulating interest in the album. Thus, while concerts continued to be sell-outs, record sales went into decline.

It's Only Rock 'n' Roll was released the following year, in October 1974. Once again, this is a Stones album that is remembered by the group's audience with little affection, and yet it contains much excellent material and is also notable for some fluid and melodic guitar artistry from Mick Taylor. The title-track, and single, was originally recorded at Ron Wood's house, with him and Jagger on guitars, Willie Weeks (bass), Kenny Jones (drums), and apparently David Bowie helping out on the chorus. The tape was then finished off in The Stones' own studio with overdubs, especially from Richard, of course.

The song itself was little more than one line of melody, somewhat artificially stretched into a complete three-minutes. The lyrics too were unsuccessful, as they tried to parody the excesses of outrage and violence to which certain stars (notably Alice Cooper) had taken rock. However, it was hardly an original theme for the time, and was being tackled simultaneously in the films such as Brian de Palma's *Phantom Of The Paradise*. The main problem was that the topic itself was such a ludicrous parody to start with that constructing a parody of that was quite superfluous.

Nevertheless, that was just one track. Many of the others, like the rippling *Time Waits For No-one*, were excellent. There was also a version of the old Temptations' number, *Ain't Too Proud To Beg*. It was a long time since The Stones had last covered a Tamla song. (The previous occasion had been in 1965: Marvin Gaye's *Hitch Hike* on *Out Of Our Heads*.)

At the end of the year The Stones assembled in Munich to begin recording a new album. Or, at least, four of them did. Mick Taylor did not join them. He suddenly announced that he was leaving the group to head in a new direction of his own. It was a shock announcement, especially since on *It's Only Rock 'n' Roll* he had finally seemed to have meshed perfectly into the group's overall sound. But in personality terms he was shy, and had never become a natural group-member. Probably he felt he'd been with them long enough and that, given their unexacting work-schedule, he could develop his career more satisfactorily on his own. (Though, if such were his plans, he failed to realise them.) Keith Richard sent Taylor a valedictory telegram which apparently brought tears to his (Taylor's) eyes.

Press speculation about his replacement immediately became rife. The Stones themselves approached the problem in a leisurely manner, and virtually turned the sessions for the next album into auditions for a new guitarist. This was wholly to the group's benefit, since the album, when it appeared, featured contributions from both Harvey Mandel and Wayne Perkins, who had emerged as the front-runners from a field that at various times was also supposed to have included Rory Gallagher, Steve Marriott, Bobby Tench and Jeff Beck. Perkins, in fact, all but landed the job; Richard had even offered him a room in his house, to facilitate extra coaching, when Ron Wood suddenly appeared in Munich.

Straightaway, Wood began to seem the natural choice. He was completely unlike Taylor. His social behaviour was on a par with the group's – and indeed, his present group, The Faces, was renowned as much for its camaraderie as its music. At first, it was simply explained that Wood would be guesting on The Stones' massive tours of the Americas, which took up the whole of June and July. Further, Wood had joined The Stones straight from a similarly-exhausting stint with The Faces. Jagger however was insistent that The Stones must not pinch a guitarist from elsewhere, thus precipitating the break-up of that band; so it was always made clear that Wood was simply guesting.

The 1975 tour provided more vintage Stones spectacles. The elaborate design of the stage meant that the group incurred huge costs. They all entered on a large revolving stage, in the shape of a star, with a group-member revealed at each of its five points when the whole thing opened up. That wasn't all, there was also a gigantic, inflated phallus, which Jagger bestrode,

not without some difficulty. He also craved the indulgence of those sitting in the most expensive seats in the front rows by throwing buckets of water over them. Basically, Jagger felt that the spectacle of The Stones' shows had to outdo everything else that was being offered on the rock circuit at the time. Other Stones were more phlegmatic about this aspect of the show; Richard would have been quite happy simply to have played the music.

The tour, in any case, was a great success, with the whole pageantry repeated across Europe the following year, when Princess Margaret attended The Stones' Wembley shows. The climax of the UK dates was a performance at Knebworth open-air concert in front of two hundred thousand people; other performers on the bill included 10cc and Todd Rundgren's Utopia.

There had been no new album to promote for the US dates, only *Made In The Shade*, an official compilation that was effectively their third volume of greatest hits; but this wholly lacked the charm and thoughtfulness that had been the hallmarks of the Decca compilations. *Made In The Shade* seemed what it undoubtedly was – an opportunist collection which no-one had bothered to plan properly.

By the time of the UK dates there was a new recording, *Black And Blue*. Also, by then, The Stones were a wholly operational five-man line-up again. In December 1975 Rod Stewart had quit The Faces to launch his solo career proper, and within a couple of days there was an official announcement from The Stones' office to the effect that Wood had filled the longstanding group vacancy. No-one was surprised, although it always seemed that one problem was that Wood, who had seemed like a minor key Richard in The Faces, might simply be duplicating what Richard was doing, and not complementing it, as Taylor had done. By now, however, Wood was placed first in a field of one. The Stones could theoretically have had whomsoever they wanted, but in practice Wood seemed the natural recruit, and Jagger and co. could no more escape that conclusion than their fans could.

Wood thus appeared on the cover of *Black And Blue*, although he was only one of three extra featured guitarists, and the group even had to announce that he appeared "by courtesy of Warner Bros. Records".

By this time, apart from the central replacement of a guitarist, there had also been other changes in The Stones' retinue. Bobby Keyes, who'd adopted the lifestyle of a Rolling Stone just a little too whole-heartedly (while on the road he would continually order champagne and caviar), and Jim Price went after the tours of 1973. Both Jimmy Miller and studio engineer Andy Johns stopped working on Stones' recordings after *Goat's Head Soup*. The group used a number of engineers, and production duties were simply incorporated into the overall work-load of Jagger and Richards, who started using the soubriquet 'Glimmer Twins' when crediting these extra functions.

Obviously, some artists who need outside guidance

tend to handicap themselves by acting as their own producers; but many of the most accomplished names in rock have never needed another pair of ears, and Jagger and Richards certainly found each other's sufficient.

The album *Black And Blue* found The Stones still extending their rhythmic range, and showing influences they'd picked up in Jamaica – although when they attempted a direct transposition of a reggae song, as in Eric Donaldson's *Cherry Oh Baby*, they were not successful. Mostly, though, the album shows the group staying alive to contemporary sounds (particularly the salsa and urban street-funk of New York) and being able to integrate them into their own well-established patterns of composition. Which, some would say, is the secret of The Stones' longevity: to blend continuity and change; to be contemporary while remaining the same.

The single from the album, *Fool To Cry* was a lachrymose, sentimental ballad – entirely untypical Stones material, though once again it seemed to find a new audience when issued as a single.

After *Black And Blue* the group owed one more piece of work under its existing contract, and it was decided to make that a live double – a reasonable decision in view of the fact that there hadn't been a live album from the band since 1970. In the meantime they – and by this time Jagger was virtually in charge of all business arrangements himself – proceeded to negotiate new contracts straightaway, publicly making known their intentions to ask for staggering advances, and explaining that they did not actually expect any record company to make money out of handling their catalogue (which, effectively, was all The Rolling Stones Records was, although one other artist was signed at this time, Peter Tosh). They would simply be, they said, a prestigious name to have on the company roster. In the end, they stayed with Atlantic for the US market, but switched to EMI in the UK.

The greatest-ever threat to the continuation of The Stones' career together occurred in February 1977, in Toronto, Canada. The group intended using performances from their 1976 European dates for the live double-album, but in order to offer the public something fresh had decided to lay down some new material in a club atmosphere. This plan went to schedule, and four of the songs recorded in Toronto's El Mocambo club – Muddy Waters' *Mannish Boy*, Chuck Berry's *Around And Around*, Bo Diddley's *Crackin' Up* and *Little Red Rooster* duly appeared on side three of *Love You Live*.

It happened prior to the club performance that all but scuttled The Stones. Keith was busted in his hotel, the Harbour Castle, by the Royal Canadian Mounted Police. He was charged not only with possession of heroin, but – such had been the quantity discovered – with trafficking as well.

Thus began a long and traumatic saga, one result of which was that Keith Richard became known as Keith Richards, since that was his real name and the name

under which charges were preferred. Richards, however, managed to avoid custodial punishment. This was largely because he and Anita voluntarily committed themselves to hospital outside New York, and made determined, successful efforts to overcome heroin addiction. Richards explained that he had first became addicted in the mid-seventies, and had generally used the drug to combat feelings of boredom and depression after the group had completed a lengthy touring itinerary.

The Canadian bench thus took a sympathetic view to Richards' plight, and by the time his case was finally heard in October 1978, there were few who expected the authorities to inflict a harsh and exemplary punishment. In the end, no prison sentence at all was imposed. Richards was merely fined, and the group was ordered to play two charity concerts in the country. This seemed a humanitarian and wholly sensible way for the judiciary to have handled the case. The Stones gratefully fulfilled the obligation placed upon them at the earliest opportunity by giving concerts for the blind at the Oshawa Civic Centre in April 1979.

Towards the end of September 1977, the group began work on the album that surfaced a year later as *Some Girls*. The vast success of the release bears out two points that have been made earlier: the first is that albums released as the first product of a new contract have commercially-enhanced prospects. In this case, *Some Girls* and its sequel, *Emotional Rescue*, became The Stones' two biggest-selling albums to date.

The second point is the indispensability of the hit single. *Some Girls* did contain a stand-out 45, *Miss You*, which showed Jagger and Richards utilising the slinky disco rhythms that were making such a contemporary impact. It raced towards the top of the charts and, though it didn't quite reach Number One, became the most successful single from the band since *Brown Sugar* in 1971.

Even apart from that one track, *Some Girls* was a fine album, which created the impression that Jagger and Richards had worked hard to lift the group's recording career to a new plateau, being aware that it was a commercially advantageous juncture to do so.

The success of *Some Girls*, however, cannot be explained by its quality alone. It can largely be attributed to the marketing push given to it, and to the commercial stimulus provided by such a huge hit single as *Miss You*. The fact that *Some Girls* is the group's most successful album, therefore, says nothing about the relative merits of Stones albums, only that marketing techniques had got that much more sophisticated by the late seventies, so that a company could maximise an album's sales potential very quickly – and this is what happened.

Previously, in fact, Stones' albums sales had belied the group's position as one of rock's pre-eminent acts, for they had not been impressive when adjudged alongside the great commercial feats of the rock business. Paul Simon once remarked, for example, that he'd never

really considered The Rolling Stones to be in the same league as Simon & Garfunkel – commercially. *Bridge Over Troubled Water* had sold millions. The sales of the best-selling Stones album (*Sticky Fingers*, at that point) only narrowly exceeded those of the worst-selling Simon & Garfunkel album (*Wednesday Morning, 3 A.M.*) – a clear demonstration that in comparison with the commercial heavyweights, The Rolling Stones were practically puny.

The re-launch of the group's career which took place when the new contract took effect in 1978 thus gave them some real commercial muscle at last. Other hits followed *Miss You* – *Beast Of Burden* also went Top Ten in the US, and *Shattered* followed it into the charts; *Respectable* became the UK follow-up single.

Some Girls featured another Stones' version of a Temptations' standard – *Just My Imagination*, and also marked the appearance on record with the group of Ian McLagan, like Ron Wood a former member of The Faces who had begun to work with The Stones on stage.

Emotional Rescue lacked the overall quality of its predecessor, and actually fared far better in the US than the UK, where it failed to generate much support. The title-track itself became a Top Ten single, though its successor, *She's So Cold*, did poorly. The album had been recorded in Paris and the Bahamas, and featured an array of guest-stars, including Max Romeo and Michael Shrieve. There were also nostalgic re-appearances from figures who'd worked with the group a decade earlier – Bobby Keyes and Nicky Hopkins, and Jack Nitzsche, who arranged the horns.

The Stones returned to the touring circuit in September 1981, in much-publicised fashion. As was by now their custom, they went through America one year, and tackled Europe the next. On the dates, the group absolutely consolidated their position as the world's leading rock 'n' roll band, playing with an exuberance and a fire hardly credible in a band that had been slogging away for twenty years. Their triumphal procession across the continents was indeed an extravagant media event, with Jagger the toast of every city in which they appeared.

There were new albums to tie in with each series of dates: a new studio effort, *Tattoo You*, arrived in time for the opening of the US tour at the John F. Kennedy stadium in Philadelphia. This showed The Stones working at a familiar level; there was nothing actually to complain about, but by their standards it was unexceptional. It was just another Stones album, with the virtues one has come to expect, but without any thrilling or innovatory qualities. *Start Me Up* became a US and UK Top 10 single; so, in the US only, did *Waiting On A Friend*.

Tapes from the US concerts were used for a live album, *Still Life (American Tour 1981)* released to coincide with the European dates the following summer. *Still Life* included material spanning most stages of the group's twenty-year history, plus a couple of rock classics – Eddie Cochran's *Twenty Flight Rock* and Smokey Robinson's *Going To A Go-Go* – that the group had not previously committed to vinyl.

There was a film of those dates, too, *Let's Spend The Night Together*, which opened in London, March 1983.

By that time, this was an unusual venture, for the group's filming activities had all but ceased. *Ladies And Gentlemen, The Rolling Stones* (1974) had been intended to be an in-depth study of the band, but those plans had gone awry, and the finished film was simply documentary footage of the group performing in Fort Worth, in 1972. (A film-maker called Robert Frank had been working on a project called *Cocksucker Blues*, which would have incorporated the *Ladies And Gentlemen* material – but, not surprisingly, perhaps, in view of its ambitious title, the project never materialised.)

In 1981 Jagger was involved in another solo venture, working with Werner Herzog on *Fitzcarraldo*. The film itself proved to be a charismatic one, but the circumstances of its shooting, in the Peruvian jungle, proved altogether too hair-raising for Mick, who departed abruptly, and thus his part was cut altogether from the completed film. Jagger still cherished dreams of somehow establishing himself in the cinema, but for both him and The Stones almost every connection with the film world seemed to have been blighted.

Mick with Pete Townshend.

Mick Jagger is a survivor. Twenty years after The Stones first sprang to public attention, he has become the world's leading rock 'n' roll personality, and at the same time one of the most sought after of *saloniers*. Is there any contradiction? Not with Jagger. Rebellion to him is a part of rock 'n' roll, and rock 'n' roll is a part of his life. It is something he does for a living. Most other people can adopt different lines of thought, and different attitudes when they go to the office or report for work. Jagger sees no reason to be different.

What is astonishing is that he has managed to retain this approach while never compromising the credibility of either himself or his group – which is especially important since he has been operating in an area where credibility is king. While others – Cliff Richard, say – have been dismissed as being culturally insignificant, Jagger has always retained his image intact. Yet in many ways Jagger is just like the Cliff Richard of the fifties, the apparent rebel whose rebelliousness could never quite be pinned down. Both were virtually clean slates, empty mirrors in which one could imagine the face of one's choosing; any would have fitted. While Richard soon developed a very definite personality, Jagger's remained elusive. He continued to practice the dictum preached forcibly by Col. Tom Parker to Elvis Presley – "say nothing and keep it dignified". Jagger, in short, has maintained his credibility by avoiding questions on virtually all real issues. The most glaring example of this was in the *Sunday Times* when John Mortimer attempted to interview him. As soon as the conversation reached sensitive areas, however, Jagger simply declined to be interviewed, refusing even to allow Mortimer to infer that he "wasn't right-wing". Jagger has never said anything that might alienate a section of his audience. He actually allows his fans to construct a Jagger personality for themselves. However they construct the pieces, Jagger can always be guaranteed to fit it.

In the case of the Mortimer interview, Jagger's evasiveness was particularly regrettable, since the former, the famous author, playwright and barrister, had played no small part in helping to defend court members of the late sixties underground with whom Jagger was thought to share some affinity. One says 'thought to' because on reflection it is clear that Jagger has hardly ever been associated with anything, and has spurned social movements as deliberately as he has shunned political campaigns.

There are obviously senses in which one regrets that Jagger has been allowed to maintain these poses, and get away with it. Paul McCartney, for example, is considered a marshmallow performer in comparison with Jagger – and yet as a soloist he has actually composed and recorded one song of political commitment, *Give Ireland Back To The Irish*. Jagger has never laid his balls on the line in such fashion.

Of course, Jagger is also widely considered one of the most glamorously sexual of performers, and on the basis of his sexuality he has always attracted a large female following – and, it must be said, a largely uncritical one. For there are few rock stars who have done more to downgrade the female sex. He has nearly always regarded women as no more than passing objects of carnal interest, and has made little attempt to disguise his contempt for the dignity of women. Yet only on rare occasions have women actually protested about his behaviour. The bondage adverts that accompanied *Black And Blue* stimulated a considerable outcry, and groups of females in the US objected to the lyrical content of *Some Girls*. But even so Jagger was able to survive such passing condemnation of his work and attitudes; there is no evidence that he incurred any long-term wrath from even militant feminists. Really, he is like jelly – it's so difficult to attack him when he never really commits himself to anything; if he is attacked, his invariable tactic is to try to sidle out of the accusation – he will never stand and defend his ground. Similarly, his own relationships with girls have never rebounded on him. Although both Marianne Faithfull and Chrissie Shrimpton attempted suicide over him, he skilfully avoided damaging personal publicity.

For such a public figure, he also manages to keep his private affairs entirely private. He has as much money as Paul McCartney, and owns as many houses as he does, yet his millions are less frequently commented upon. Over the years he has discovered how to handle the press. Now, his relationship with Jerry Hall attracts only minimal interest. Jagger knows he can expect photographers and a media buzz when he goes to particular places (clubs, mostly) so he tends to avoid them. Occasionally media flare-ups are unavoidable – there was one in December 1982 when Jerry Hall temporarily left him and walked off with millionaire racehorse-owner Robert Sangster – but they quickly die down. Jagger ensures that they are starved of the necessary fuel (i.e. further pieces of gossip) to sustain them.

His business affairs are similarly protected from public scrutiny; Prince Rupert Loewenstein arranges all financial matters for him and the group. Jagger always insists that he is not interested in personal possessions, and has only a few, but it is known that he is building his own art collection. On the whole, though, how he invests and disposes of his great wealth are matters of

which he manages to keep the public totally uninformed.

The strange thing about Jagger is that even when he does lift a corner of the veil and make an honest statement, few people seem to believe him. He has said, for example, that he only entered the rock business for the money, and this is probably true. Indeed, he has sometimes been candid on the point, explaining that actually wanting money is perhaps not such a bad thing – after all, there is a purpose behind it. It might perhaps be far worse to desire intangible things, like adulation.

However it is very easy to mock Jagger (and mockery after all is one of his own standard ploys). Finally, though, one must respect him as a survivor. One may denigrate his methods; one may even denigrate his character – but fame is a particularly vicious double-edged sword, and the full glare of media attention, which Jagger has had to endure often enough, can burn people out and destroy them. It is necessary to find ways of protecting oneself. Jagger has protected himself by putting on different faces, and keeping his own hidden; or at best revealing his own nature merely as one of a number of personalities, leaving all guessing about which is the real one.

It is true that many in the rock audience almost do expect their stars to destroy themselves for their art; self-sacrifice becomes the highest level of performance.

There are many who have obliged. Jagger was never one of them – he never took rock 'n' roll that seriously. Certainly, after everything suddenly seemed to him to possess too much reality, after Altamont, he changed direction, and emasculated his lyrics. That is why Altamont was so important – when it seemed that Jagger's art and Jagger's life were becoming too closely entangled, he immediately pulled back from the brink, and divested his art of all real meaning. Since Altamont, the words of all Rolling Stones' songs have been, deliberately, wholly insignificant.

To him, rock 'n' roll was never a way of life – it was simply a way of earning a living. His commitment has been strictly finite. It is this which has sustained him, and allowed him to endure and survive: the evergreen performer, the prince of showmen, rock's own solid rock.

NOTE

In 1977, after his arrest on serious drugs charges in Toronto, Keith Richard was charged under his real name of Keith Richards. The following year, to clarify a growing confusion in the press, he announced that in future he would prefer to be known by his real name. His record company, EMI, issued a press release to this effect.

To avoid a similar confusion, therefore, and also to avoid re-writing history, this book makes the change of surname at the same moment that Keith himself requested it. Thus, he is referred to as 'Richard' until the Toronto events, and 'Richards' thereafter.

The U.S. tour, 1981. Top left: Philadelphia; bottom left: New Jersey Arena; bottom right: a duet with Tina Turner.

DISCOGRAPHY

Discography   The Rolling Stones

The Rolling Stones *(Decca 1964)*
Rolling Stones No.2 *(Decca 1965)*
Out Of Our Heads *(Decca 1965)*
Aftermath *(Decca 1966)*
Between The Buttons *(Decca 1967)*
Their Satanic Majesties Request *(Decca 1967)*
Beggar's Banquet *(Decca 1968)*
Let It Bleed *(Decca 1969)*
Get Yer Ya-Ya's Out *(Decca 1970)*
Sticky Fingers *(Rolling Stones 1971)*
Exile On Main Street *(Rolling Stones 1972)*
Goat's Head Soup *(Rolling Stones 1973)*
It's Only Rock 'n' Roll *(Rolling Stones 1974)*
Black And Blue *(Rolling Stones 1976)*
Love You Live *(Rolling Stones 1977)*
Some Girls *(Rolling Stones 1978)*
Emotional Rescue *(Rolling Stones 1980)*
Tattoo You *(Rolling Stones 1981)*
Still Life *(Rolling Stones 1982)*

OFFICIAL COMPILATIONS

Big Hits (High Tide And Green Grass) *(Decca 1966)*
Through The Past, Darkly *(Decca 1969)*
Made In The Shade *(Rolling Stones 1975)*
Time Waits For No-One *(Rolling Stones 1979)*
Sucking In The Seventies *(Rolling Stones 1981)*

CONTRIBUTIONS TO:

Thank Your Lucky Stars, Vol. 2 *(Decca 1963)*
Ready, Steady, Go! *(Decca 1964)*
Saturday Club *(Decca 1964)*
Fourteen *(Decca 1964)*

EPs

The Rolling Stones *(Decca 1964)*
Five By Five *(Decca 1964)*
Got Live If You Want It *(Decca 1965)*

UNAUTHORISED COMPILATIONS

Stone Age *(Decca 1971)*
Milestones *(Decca 1972)*
Gimme Shelter *(Decca 1972)*
Rock 'n' Rolling Stones *(Decca 1972)*
No Stone Unturned *(Decca 1973)*
Metamorphosis *(Decca 1975)*
Rolled Gold *(Decca 1975)*

MICK JAGGER

Performance (soundtrack) *(Warner Bros. 1970)*

Also:

Nicky Hopkins, Ry Cooder, Mick Jagger, Bill Wyman & Charlie Watts: Jamming with Edward (Rolling Stones 1972)

PROTEUS ROCKS

The Best Rock 'n' Roll Reading from Proteus

☐ **TOYAH**
An illustrated fan's eyeview much-liked by Toyah herself.
by Gaynor Evans
UK £1.95
US $3.95

☐ **REGGAE: DEEP ROOTS MUSIC**
The definitive history of reggae. A major TV tie-in.
by Howard Johnson and Jim Pines
UK £5.95
US $10.95

☐ **BOOKENDS**
The first full study of Simon and Garfunkel, their joint and solo careers.
by Patrick Humphries
UK £5.95
US $10.95

☐ **PRETENDERS**
The first full study of this powerful and turbulent band.
by Chris Salewicz
UK £3.95
US $7.95

☐ **LOU REED**
A definitive profile of this almost reclusive figure.
by Diana Clapton
UK £4.95
US $9.95.

☐ **JAMES LAST**
A fully illustrated study of this world phenomenon of popular music.
by Howard Elson
UK £4.95
US $9.95

☐ **RARE RECORDS**
A complete illustrated guide to wax trash and vinyl treasures.
by Tom Hibbert
UK £4.95
US $9.95

☐ **THE PERFECT COLLECTION**
The 200 greatest albums, the 100 greatest singles selected and discussed by leading rock journalists.
Edited by Tom Hibbert
UK £4.95
US $9.95

☐ **EARLY ROCKERS**
All the seminal figures of rock 'n' roll:
Berry, Little Richard, Jerry Lee, Presley et al.
by Howard Elson
UK £4.95
US $9.95

KATE BUSH ☐
Complete illustrated story of this unique artist.
by Paul Kerton
UK £3.95
US $7.95

BLACK SABBATH ☐
Heavy Metal Superstars.
by Chris Welch
UK £4.95
US $9.95

A-Z OF ROCK GUITARISTS ☐
First illustrated encyclopaedia of guitar greats.
by Chris Charlesworth
UK £5.95
US $10.95

A-Z OF ROCK DRUMMERS ☐
Over 300 great drummers in this companion to ROCK GUITARISTS.
by Harry Shapiro
UK £5.95
US $10.95

CHUCK BERRY ☐
The definitive biography of the original Mr Rock 'n' Roll.
by Krista Reese
UK £4.95
US $8.95

A CASE OF MADNESS ☐
A big illustrated guide for fans of this insane band.
by Mark Williams
UK only £1.95

TALKING HEADS ☐
The only illustrated book about one of the most innovative bands of the 70s and 80s.
by Krista Reese
UK £4.95
US $9.95

DURAN DURAN ☐
The best-selling illustrated biography.
UK £1.95
US $3.95

A TOURIST'S GUIDE TO JAPAN ☐
Beautifully illustrated study of Sylvian and his colleagues.
by Arthur A. Pitt.
UK £1.95
US $3.95

ILLUSTRATED POP QUIZ ☐
Over 400 impossible questions for pop geniuses only.
by Dafydd Rees and Barry Lazell
UK £2.95
US $5.95

order form overleaf